THE BIG BOOK OF
ANIMAL LIFE

SMITHMARK

MARK LAMBERT

SMITHMARK

This edition published in 1991 by SMITHMARK Publishers Inc.,
112 Madison Avenue, New York, NY 10016
By arrangement with Reed International Books
Michelin House, 81 Fulham Road, London SW3 6RB

ISBN 0-8317-0850-6

Printed in Italy

SMITHMARK Books are available for bulk purchase
for sales promotion and premium use.
For details write or telephone the Manager of Special Sales,
SMITHMARK Publishers Inc., 112 Madison Avenue,
New York, NY 10016. (212) 532-6600

CONTENTS

CELLS AND LIFE

Living organisms have seven features that distinguish them from non-living things. These are feeding, respiration (breathing), growth, excretion (getting rid of waste), movement, sensitivity and reproduction.

Animals feed by taking in plant or animal material from outside their bodies. To obtain food animals need to move. Many travel from place to place. Others, such as some sea animals, remain fixed in one place. They use movement to create water currents that bring food particles to them. Movement requires the use of sense systems to detect food and avoid obstacles and predators.

Animals also need energy to live. The energy is obtained by chemical reactions in the body that break down food. This process is called respiration, which usually needs oxygen. This oxygen is taken from the surrounding air or water.

Some food materials are also used for growth and repairing damaged tissue. Unwanted food materials and the waste products of the body's chemical processes are generally expelled from the body by a process called excretion.

All these features are designed to make possible the most important feature of living things – reproduction. To make sure each kind of animal continues to exist, new individuals must be produced to replace those that die.

The cell is the basic unit of every living organism. Some organisms consist of just one cell, others consist of hundreds or even millions of cells. Each cell consists of a watery fluid, called cytoplasm, surrounded by a thin membrane.

Birds, such as this Golden eagle, use up a great deal of energy when flying. They obtain this energy by eating large amounts of food, some of which they convert into energy using the oxygen they breathe in from the air.

A starfish, like all living organisms, feeds, grows and reproduces. It "breathes" oxygen from the water, moves, and uses senses to detect things around it.

Inside the cell is a nucleus. This controls the working of many tiny structures called organelles. Each organelle carries out one of the basic functions of the cell. The mitochondria, for example, are used for respiration and energy production. The Golgi body is involved in waste disposal. The endoplasmic reticulum helps make proteins which are then used by the cell for growth.

Overall growth of an organism is achieved by cell division. Often there are special cells that enable an animal to reproduce itself. Other specialized cells are involved in movement and sense systems.

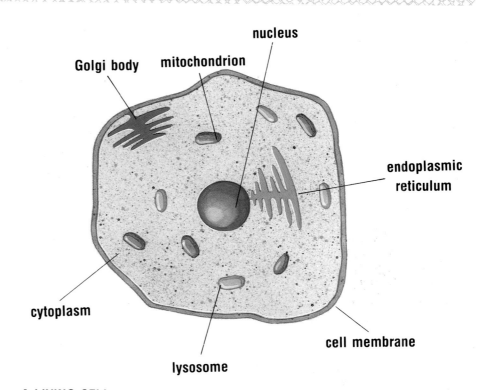

nucleus

Golgi body   **mitochondrion**

endoplasmic reticulum

cytoplasm

cell membrane

lysosome

A LIVING CELL

Impala get the energy they need from plants. The waste materials impalas excrete are broken down by bacteria and the chemicals are then reused by plants.

Fish, such as this salmon, get the oxygen they need from the water around them. Like most other animals, fish have complex nervous systems.

THE ANIMAL KINGDOM

Animals vary enormously in size and complexity. At one extreme are the single-celled animals, such as the amoebae. At the other extreme is the blue whale, the largest mammal that has ever existed. In between are more than 1 million animals that scientists know about, and possibly several million more that have not yet been discovered.

To help understand this huge collection of animals and the relationships between them, scientists use a system of classification. The animals are divided into groups and sub-groups.

The main divisions of the animal kingdom are called phyla. "Phyla" is the plural form of the word "phylum." All the vertebrates (animals with backbones) belong to one phylum. It is called the Chordata (see page 14).

Invertebrates (animals without backbones) are divided into 23 phyla. This means vertebrates are more closely related to each other than, say, the flatworms and the roundworms. These two groups of invertebrates form separate phyla.

In each phylum, there may be several sub-groups. Each sub-group is divided into yet more sub-groups. The main sub-groups for classifying animals, in descending order, are: the class, order and family. Other sub-groups, such as the subclass, superorder, suborder, superfamily and subfamily, are also used for greater distinction.

In each family or subfamily animals are classified as genera. Each genus contains one or more species. The species is the lowest sub-group. Members of the same species can interbreed successfully with each other but not normally with members of other species.

Animals are often known by their common names, but these often vary around the world, and give no indication of the connection between closely related species. For scientific purposes, animals are given Latin-style scientific names. Each name has two parts. The first part indicates the genus. The second part indicates the species. A lion's scientific name, for example, is *Panthera leo*, and the tiger's name is *Panthera tigris*. These names indicate that the animals are different species belonging to the same genus.

Animalia								Kingdom
Chordata								Phylum
Craniata								Subphylum
Mammalia								Class
Artiodactyla								Order
Bovidae								Family
Gazella								Genus
Gazella thomsoni								Species

In the modern system of classification, animals are grouped together according to their similarity. All animals belong to the Kingdom Animalia, but only those that have a notochord (a stiff, rod-like structure) at some stage of their lives belong to the Phylum Chordata. Each lower group defines a smaller number of animals. The genus *Gazella*, for example, contains just 2 species.

Opposite: The barred leaf-folding frog is found in the rainforests of Central and South Americas.

ANIMALS WITHOUT BACKBO

Most of the approximately 1.4 million known species of animal belong to the 23 phyla of invertebrates (these are animals without backbones).

The simplest invertebrates are the protozoans, of which there are some 30,000 species. They are a varied group of single-celled animals that includes the amoebas, ciliates like *Paramecium* and *Stentor*, shelled forms called radiolarians and foraminiferans and single-celled parasites. (Parasites are organisms that live at the expense of others, see page 70.) A well-known one is *Plasmodium*, the malaria parasite.

Many-celled invertebrates include the sponges (about 30,000 species), coelenterates (corals, jellyfish and sea anemones; about 9,000 species), flatworms (10,000 species), roundworms (17,000 species) and a number of smaller phyla, such as the moss animals, ribbon-worms, thorny-headed worms, lamp shells, peanut worms and water bears.

Earthworms belong to the phylum known as the Annelida, or segmented worms. This phylum also contains leeches and a number of sea-living worms, such as ragworms and fanworms.

One of the largest phyla is that of the mollusks, which contains over 75,000 species. This group includes snails, slugs and their relatives, bivalves such as mussels, clams and cockles, and the tentacled mollusks such as octopuses, squid and cuttlefish.

The echinoderms ("spiny skins") form another phylum. This phylum includes the starfish, sea urchins, sea cucumbers, sea lilies and brittle-stars.

The largest phylum of all is that of the Arthropoda, a name that means "jointed foot." All members of this group have hard outer skeletons, and they walk on legs that have several joints. Living members of the Arthropoda include the arachnids (spiders and their relatives; 50,000 species), the centipedes (2,000 species), millipedes (8,000 species) and crustaceans (crabs, lobsters and shrimps; 30,000 species).

The largest class of arthropods, however, is that of the insects. There are over 1 million insect species in the world. All the flies, butterflies, wasps, bees, beetles, grasshoppers, bugs, lice and fleas are in this group.

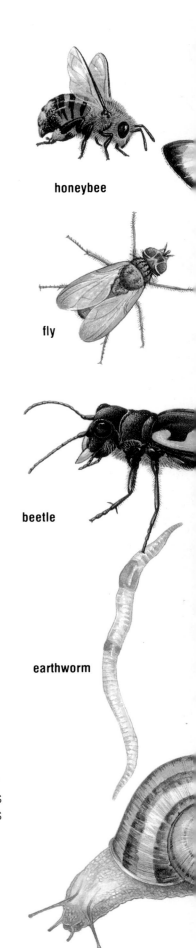

honeybee

fly

beetle

earthworm

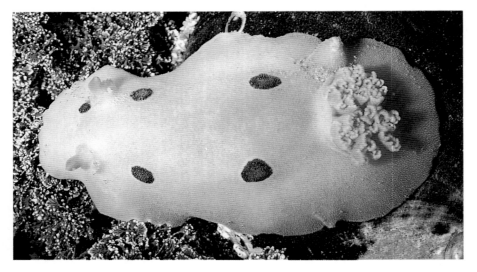

Left: A sea slug crawls across the bottom of a pool at low tide. As their name implies, sea slugs are related to land slugs and snails.

NES

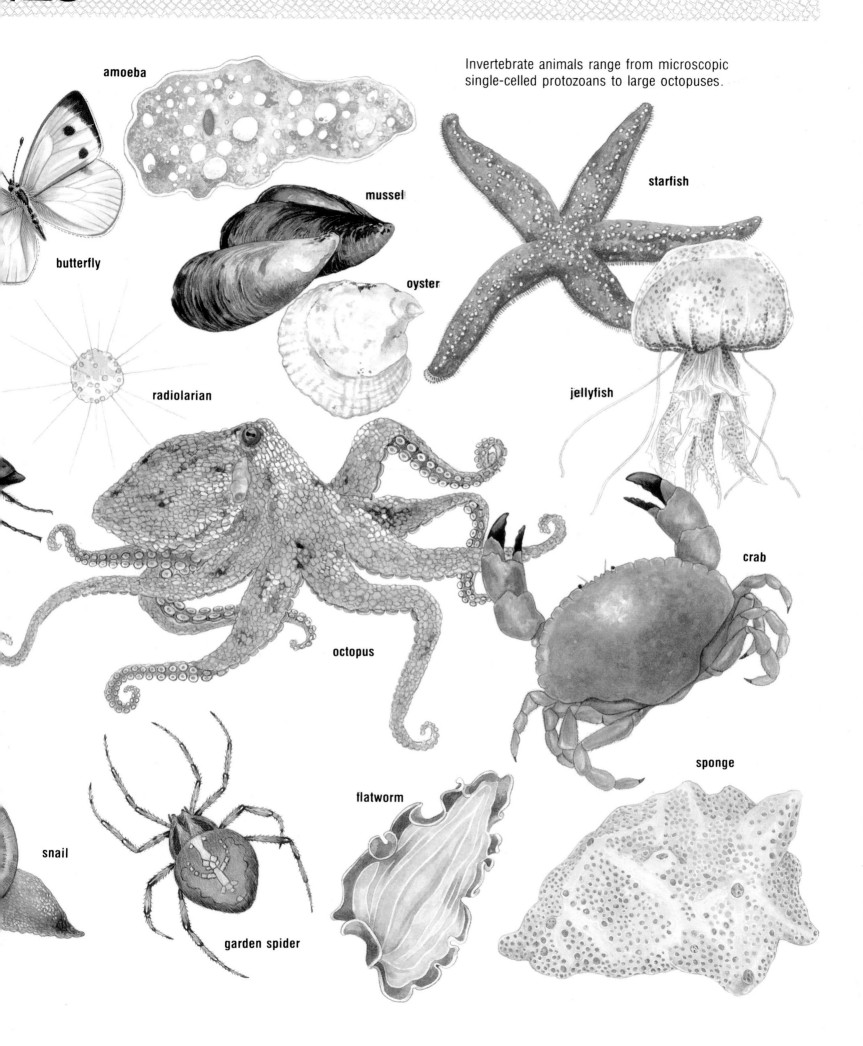

amoeba

Invertebrate animals range from microscopic single-celled protozoans to large octopuses.

butterfly

mussel

starfish

oyster

radiolarian

jellyfish

octopus

crab

sponge

snail

flatworm

garden spider

13

ANIMALS WITH BACKBONE

There are only about 40,000 species of backboned animals. They are called vertebrates, and they are generally considered to be more advanced than animals without backbones. Backboned animals belong to the phylum Chordata, a group that also includes the sea squirts and the fish-like lancelets.

The most primitive of the vertebrates are the two groups of jawless fish, the hags and the lampreys. Next are the sharks and rays, which are distinguished by having internal skeletons made of a gristly material called cartilage. All other vertebrates have skeletons made of bones.

Bony fishes form a much larger, more varied class. Their success is due partly to the fact that they have more mobile jaws so they can nibble food. They also have gas-filled bags in their bodies that enable them to float in the water.

The amphibians – frogs, toads, newts and salamanders – are a group that represents the emergence of vertebrates onto land. Unlike fishes, amphibians have legs for walking. Some amphibians even live permanently out of the water. All amphibians, however, need moist conditions to breed, and most return to water to lay their eggs.

On the other hand, reptiles – lizards, snakes, crocodiles and tortoises – are true land animals. They have scaly, waterproof skins, and they lay leathery eggs in which the young develop. Birds lay similar hard-shelled eggs, but birds have feathers instead of scales. Birds have also acquired the ability to use their forelimbs as wings for flying.

Birds are also warm-blooded animals. This means they keep their bodies at a constant temperature by using the heat

Right: The collared lizard is a typical reptile. It is found in the southwestern part of the U.S.A. It feeds on insects and other, smaller, lizards.

Below: Vertebrate animals all belong to one phylum. There are five classes–fishes, amphibians, reptiles, birds and mammals.

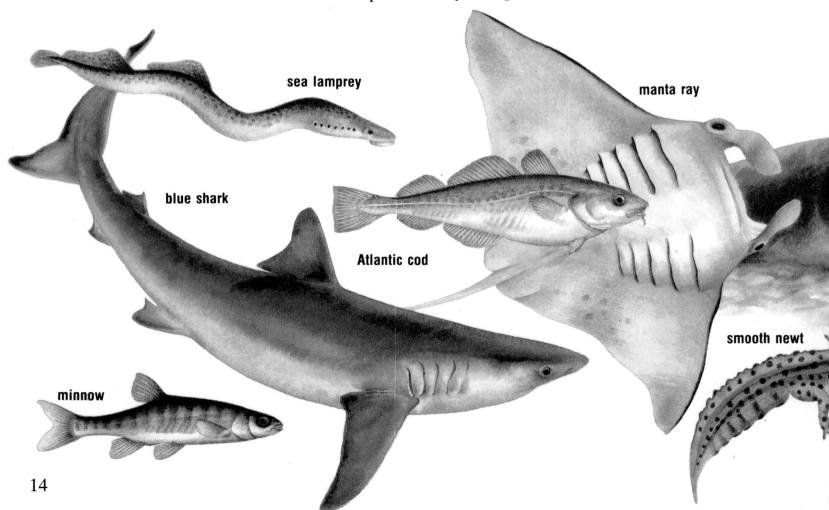

sea lamprey

manta ray

blue shark

Atlantic cod

smooth newt

minnow

generated by chemical processes inside their bodies. Feathers also help to keep them warm.

Mammals, are warm-blooded animals as well, but they have fur or hair to keep them warm. Mammals do not lay eggs. Instead the young develop inside their mother's body until they are relatively well developed. After the babies are born they are suckled. This means they feed on milk produced by glands in the mother's skin.

Californian condor

cheetah and cub

Californian sea lion

crocodile

common viper or adder

15

EVOLUTION

Most people believe that the living things we see today have evolved gradually over millions of years. This is known as the Theory of Evolution. This theory was first put forward by the English naturalist Charles Darwin in 1859 in his book, *On the Origin of Species by Means of Natural Selection*.

Darwin began to work out his ideas about evolution on a voyage to the Galapagos Islands in the Pacific Ocean. The animals he saw there were very different from the animals he had seen on the mainland. Yet, the animals on the islands had almost certainly descended from animals on the mainland, Darwin thought. The animals on the island had adapted to the local conditions, and, in some cases, several different species had evolved from a common ancestor. Today, similar examples of evolution exist in isolated places.

There is other evidence that supports Darwin's theory. Much of this evidence comes from the study of fossils. These are the remains of animals and plants that lived millions of years ago, and some fossils clearly demonstrate stages during the evolutionary process. Fossils of *Archaeopteryx*, the first-known bird, for example, have features like those of reptiles. This supports the widely held belief that birds have evolved from reptiles.

There is also evidence of evolution in living animals. When different animals have similar features, this indicates they may have once had a common ancestor. The various kinds of legs, flippers and wings that are found among

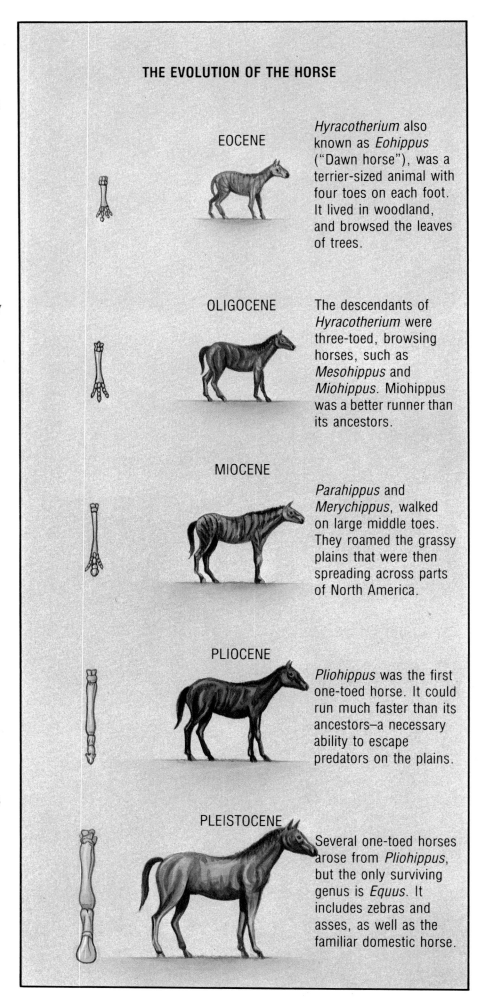

THE EVOLUTION OF THE HORSE

EOCENE

Hyracotherium also known as *Eohippus* ("Dawn horse"), was a terrier-sized animal with four toes on each foot. It lived in woodland, and browsed the leaves of trees.

OLIGOCENE

The descendants of *Hyracotherium* were three-toed, browsing horses, such as *Mesohippus* and *Miohippus*. Miohippus was a better runner than its ancestors.

MIOCENE

Parahippus and *Merychippus*, walked on large middle toes. They roamed the grassy plains that were then spreading across parts of North America.

PLIOCENE

Pliohippus was the first one-toed horse. It could run much faster than its ancestors—a necessary ability to escape predators on the plains.

PLEISTOCENE

Several one-toed horses arose from *Pliohippus*, but the only surviving genus is *Equus*. It includes zebras and asses, as well as the familiar domestic horse.

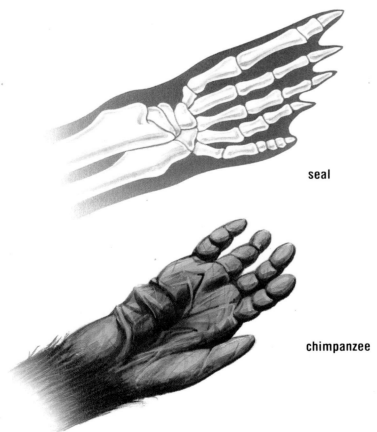

seal

chimpanzee

Left: The internal arrangement of the bones inside a seal's flipper shows it probably has the same origin as the 5 fingered hand of a chimpanzee.

Above: Przewalski's horse, the last remaining wild horse, is extinct in its natural habitat in Mongolia, but scientists hope to re-establish it.

vertebrates, for example, are all based on the same structure of a five-fingered limb.

The Theory of Evolution is constantly being reviewed and modified. According to one recently proposed idea, evolution progresses in a series of jumps or stages, rather than proceeding gradually and smoothly. This is known as the "punctuated equilibria" theory.

Yet, however evolution actually works, it is certain that the organisms we know today have evolved over millions of years.

NATURAL SELECTION

Before Charles Darwin published his ideas on evolution, he spent 22 years working out how evolution happens. Why and how did species change? Gradually, he realized species evolve by a process he called natural selection.

Individuals vary, and it is this variation that allows evolution to take place, according to Darwin's Theory of Evolution. The characteristics of each individual are determined by the genetic material in the nuclei of its cells (see page 9). Each characteristic is controlled by a small piece of genetic material called a gene.

Sometimes changes take place in the genes of sex cells. These changes are called mutations. The mutations take place in the genes of sex cells, then appear as new characteristics in an offspring. Major mutations are usually harmful. This means the mutations make it difficult, or even impossible, for the new individual to survive or reproduce successfully. Minor mutations, however, may be passed on to the next generation.

Natural selection works by acting upon such changes in a population of animals or plants. Mutations usually tend to be a disadvantage. Animals that possess mutations may be less able to compete for food and living space. Some mutations make individuals which are better adapted to their environment than others, and these individuals tend to survive. This is the way nature selects the animals and plants most suited to the environmental conditions at a particular time.

Evolution, and, therefore,

The long neck of a giraffe is the result of natural selection. Those individuals born with slightly longer necks than others were able to reach higher for food and tended to survive more easily.

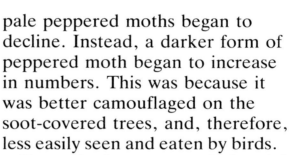

Where trees are darkened by soot, natural selection favors the darker form of peppered moth (above). In unpolluted areas, the light form (right) is more numerous.

natural selection, normally takes place very slowly. But there are examples that show how natural selection works. The best known is the example of the peppered moth. There are two forms of these moths. The normal pale peppered moth is well camouflaged on the bark of trees. But, during the Industrial Revolution, when the trees in industrial areas became covered in soot, the number of pale peppered moths began to decline. Instead, a darker form of peppered moth began to increase in numbers. This was because it was better camouflaged on the soot-covered trees, and, therefore, less easily seen and eaten by birds.

Recently, however, as industrial areas have become cleaner, light-colored peppered moths have increased in numbers, and dark moths have declined.

Stick insects are superbly camouflaged. Over millions of years, natural selection has ensured that the most stick-like of these insects are the ones that survive to reproduce.

PREHISTORIC LIFE

PALEOZOIC

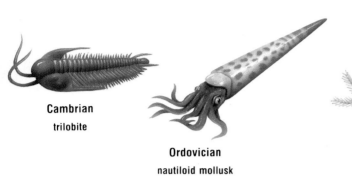

Cambrian
trilobite

Ordovician
nautiloid mollusk

Silurian
sea lily

Devonian
lungfish

Carboniferous
an early amphibian

Permian
an early shark

Life on Earth began about 3,500 million years ago. Because the history of life on Earth covers such a long time, scientists divide it into periods.

The first cells formed in the chemically rich seas that existed about 3,500 million years ago. The first living organisms were probably bacteria. They, in turn, gave rise to the first single-celled plants and animals. Many-celled organisms then evolved. By about 600 million years ago, when the Cambrian period began, there was a variety of soft-bodied creatures in the world's seas.

At this stage the first shelled animals appeared. We know this because, unlike soft-bodied animals, their remains were easily fossilized. During the next 40 million years many kinds of mollusks appeared, together with early forms of corals, primitive echinoderms and arthropods, such as crustaceans (crabs, lobsters, shrimps) and trilobites (having a three-lobed body).

The first-known vertebrates were jawless fishes, which appeared about 510 million years ago. They were followed about 70 million years later by fishes with jaws, which became widespread during the Devonian period. This was 410-355 million years ago.

Meanwhile, the first amphibians had appeared. Then, later during the Carboniferous period, 355-290 million years ago, the amphibians gave rise to the first reptiles.

By the end of what is known as the Paleozoic ("old life") era, 250 million years ago, reptiles were firmly established on land. They dominated the next 185 million years. This period is called the Mesozoic ("middle life") era, and is known as the age of reptiles.

During the Mesozoic era dinosaurs ruled the land, pterosaurs ruled the air and the seas abounded with such creatures as plesiosaurs and ichthyosaurs. All these creatures, however, became extinct about 65 million years ago, toward the end of the Mesozoic era.

The first shrew-like mammals had already appeared at the start of the Mesozoic era, but when the only ruling reptiles left were the crocodiles, mammals began to evolve and spread rapidly. The Cenozoic ("new life") era was and still is the age of the mammals. The first humans appeared on Earth about 4 million years ago.

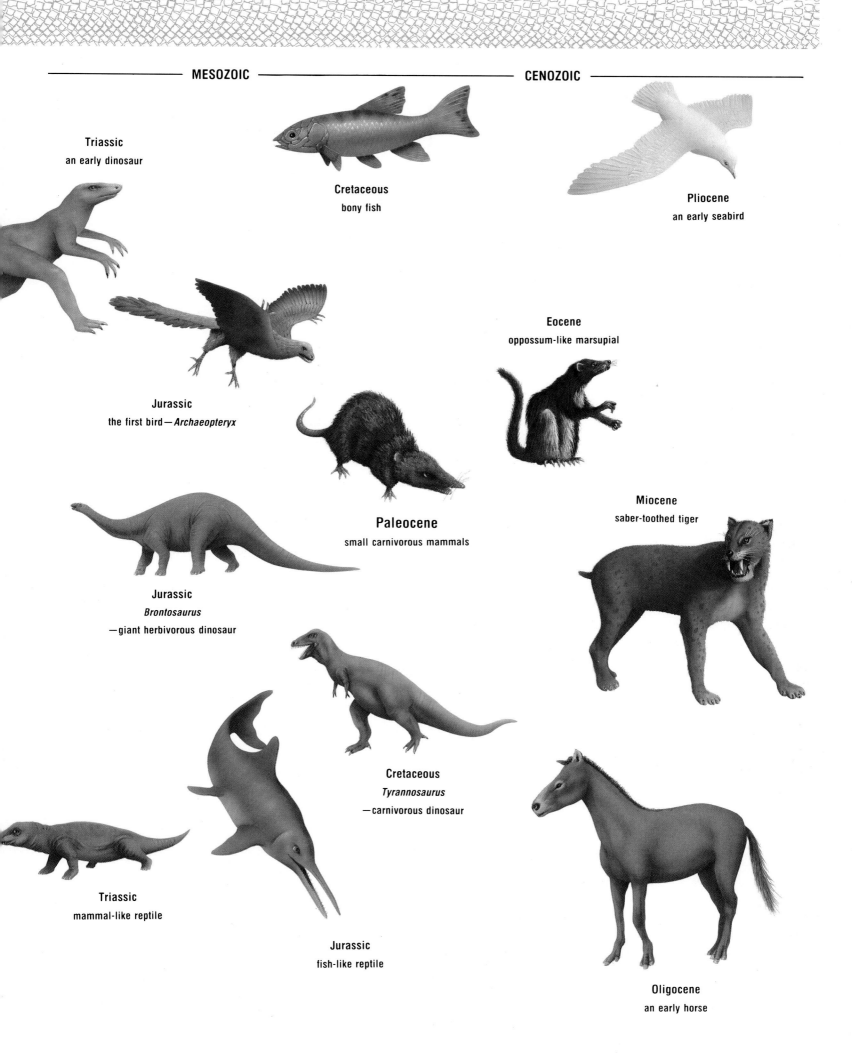

MESOZOIC — CENOZOIC —

Triassic
an early dinosaur

Cretaceous
bony fish

Pliocene
an early seabird

Jurassic
the first bird—*Archaeopteryx*

Eocene
oppossum-like marsupial

Paleocene
small carnivorous mammals

Miocene
saber-toothed tiger

Jurassic
Brontosaurus
—giant herbivorous dinosaur

Cretaceous
Tyrannosaurus
—carnivorous dinosaur

Triassic
mammal-like reptile

Jurassic
fish-like reptile

Oligocene
an early horse

HOW ANIMALS BREATHE

Unlike land mammals, a dolphin breathes air into its lungs through a single opening on the top of its head.

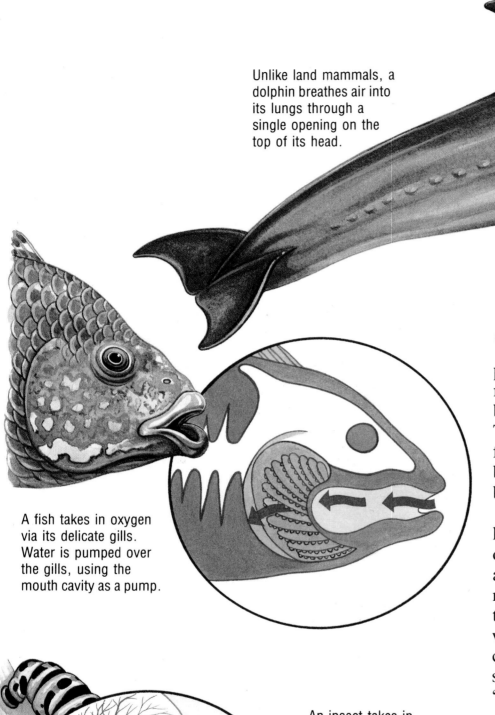

A fish takes in oxygen via its delicate gills. Water is pumped over the gills, using the mouth cavity as a pump.

An insect takes in oxygen through tiny spiracles on its sides. These lead to a system of tubes called tracheae.

spiracle

tracheae

Oxygen is vital to animals. It is used in their bodies in the process of respiration. During respiration, food is chemically broken down to release energy. This energy is then used by animals for movement and, in warm-blooded animals, for maintaining body temperature.

All animals must, therefore, have some means of obtaining oxygen. Oxygen dissolves in water and can pass through thin membranes. The simplest animals take in oxygen directly from the water around them. Protozoans, corals, flatworms and other small, soft-bodied water-dwellers all "breathe" this way.

Larger water-dwelling animals have special organs for taking in oxygen. These are known as gills. Gills are parts of the body where blood vessels lie very close to the surface, separated from the water by only a thin membrane. Gills are often folded, or feather-like, to expose the greatest possible surface area to the oxygen-giving water. Fish, crustaceans, mollusks and some amphibians, particularly the young forms, all have gills.

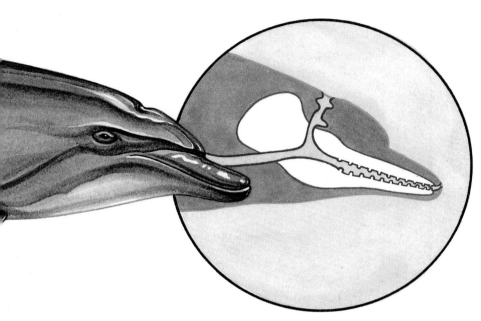

A land mammal, such as a gorilla, breathes air into a pair of lungs via its nose and mouth.

Land animals obtain their oxygen from the air, but it must be dissolved in water before it can be taken into the body. Earthworms have moist skins and can therefore take in oxygen in much the same way as their sea-living relatives. Other land-dwellers keep their moist, oxygen-absorbing surfaces protected inside their bodies. Insects, for example, take in oxygen through tiny holes called spiracles. Spiracles lead to water-filled tubes, called tracheae. An amphibian takes in some oxygen through its skin, but it also takes oxygen in through the lining of its mouth and the lining of the lung.

A land snail also has a lung, and a spider has gill-like organs called book-lungs. But the most efficient lungs are those in the more advanced vertebrates – reptiles, birds and mammals.

In a mammal, muscular action causes air to be drawn into a lung. The lung's internal surface area is vastly increased by being divided into millions of tiny sacs called alveoli. Here, oxygen dissolves in moisture and passes through the lining into the animal's blood.

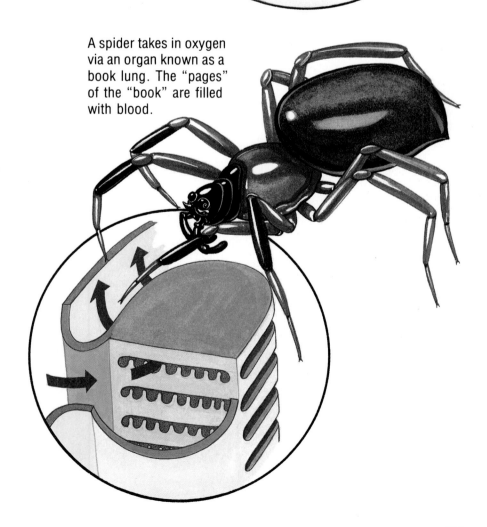

A spider takes in oxygen via an organ known as a book lung. The "pages" of the "book" are filled with blood.

PLANT EATERS

The world's plants are a rich source of food, and many animals take advantage of this. Leaves, stems, roots, fruits and seeds are all food for animals.

Grass and the leaves of trees and bushes provide food for many different animals. Plant cells, however, are surrounded by tough walls that are made of a material called cellulose. Cellulose is hard to digest and most plant-eating animals have devised special ways of dealing with it. Cattle, sheep, goats, deer, antelope, giraffe and camels are ruminants. This means they have four-chambered stomachs, one of which is called the rumen. The stomachs contain bacteria and protozoans that break

Above: Every part of a plant provides food for animals. Here, a white-eared hummingbird hovers in front of a lobelia flower to drink nectar.

sheep

peacock butterfly

down cellulose. To help the breakdown process, small lumps of partly digested food, called cud, return to the mouth from a stomach chamber to be chewed a second time for easier digestion.

Plant-eating mammals have large teeth with broad, flat crowns that grind food to a pulp as it is chewed. Sharp incisor (cutting) teeth at the front of the mouth enable mammals to bite off mouthfuls of food.

Other animals have special ways of coping with plant food. Termites have protozoans in their systems that help digest wood. A caterpillar produces enzymes that break down cellulose. Part of a grasshopper's gut is especially designed to grind tough cell walls into a pulp.

Other plant-eating animals avoid the problem by selecting the more easily digested parts of plants. Many insects, such as butterflies, moths and bees, and some birds and mammals feed on sap, nectar, fruit and seeds.

Animals are often especially adapted for feeding on particular foods. Nectar-feeding insects, for example, have a long tube, called a proboscis, for reaching deep into flowers. Nectar-feeding mammals have long tongues, and hummingbirds have long beaks as well. Sap-sucking insects have needle-like mouthparts for piercing plant stems. Seed-eating birds have short, stout beaks for cracking open the outer shells of seeds.

Below: Plant-eating animals are found in nearly every animal group. Roots, stems, leaves, buds and flowers are sources of food and different animals exploit different parts of plants.

elephant

blackbird

aphids

elephant hawkmoth
caterpillar

MEAT EATERS

Animals that eat other animals are called carnivores. Carnivores generally have to kill or capture their prey. They have evolved a wide variety of methods of doing this.

Some animals lie in wait for their victims. Web-spinning spiders, for example, catch their victims in their silken traps. Hunting spiders, on the other hand, simply run after their prey. The bolas spider uses a weapon; it hurls a sticky blob on the end of a silken thread at its victim, and this prevents the victim from escaping.

There are also mammals, such as leopards, that patiently lie in wait for potential victims. Others, such as the tiger, lion and cheetah stalk their prey and catch it with a last-minute rush. Yet others, such as the wolf and the hyena, chase their quarry until it is exhausted and then make the kill.

Carnivorous animals employ a variety of weapons to catch and kill their prey. Teeth and claws are commonly used. Carnivorous mammals, for example, have sharp, pointed canine ("dog") teeth for holding prey. Behind the canine teeth are slicing teeth that cut through flesh very easily. The claws of such animals are often sharp.

Fishes, amphibians and reptiles also use their teeth for grabbing prey. Flesh-eating birds have claws, called talons, and sharp, curved beaks for tearing flesh. Other birds have beaks designed to probe for insects or to catch fish. The mouthparts of many insects are designed to chew up the prey.

Many animals prey on species larger than themselves, so their victims must therefore be killed or subdued rapidly. Some fishes produce electric shocks to kill or stun their victims.

Other animals use poison. Poisonous snakes have special grooved teeth, called fangs, for injecting venom into the prey. Spiders also have poison fangs, and a scorpion injects poison from a tail gland. A cone shell, a type of mollusk, has a poisonous tooth on the end of a long tentacle-like proboscis. A sea anemone uses stinging cells on its tentacles to catch prey.

Meat-eaters have pointed teeth for holding and tearing. A mammal carnivore (left and below) also has slicing teeth. A snake (right) uses its fangs to inject venom. A shark (below right) can only tear at its victims.

An osprey catches fish using its sharp talons. Its hooked beak is used for tearing off pieces of flesh.

A boa constrictor kills its prey by squeezing it so tightly that it cannot breathe. The boa then swallows its victim whole.

A sea anemone catches fish and other small animals in its tentacles, which are equipped with stinging cells.

A starfish feeds on shellfish or the remains of dead sea animals, such as crabs.

MOVING IN WATER

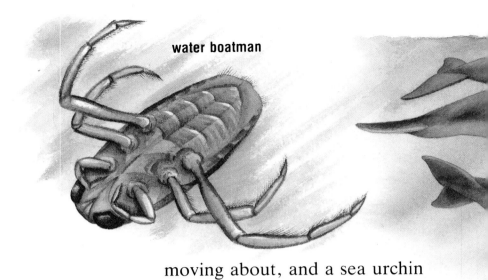

water boatman

Living in water has advantages and disadvantages for animals. Water is more dense than air. That makes water more difficult to move through than air. On the other hand, water provides more support than air. This means animals can float in water, but not in air, so less effort is needed to overcome the effects of gravity.

Some animals that live in water remain in one place all their adult lives. They often produce young forms called larvae that swim, but the movement of the adults may be restricted to swaying movements of their bodies. In many cases, tiny beating hairs, called cilia, create water currents that carry food particles to the animals.

Other water dwellers move slowly across the surface of rocks, mud or weeds. A sea snail, such as cowrie, dog whelk or topshell, has a large muscular foot. Waves of muscular contraction pass along the foot and push the animal forward. Flatworms move about in much the same way. A starfish uses tiny, fluid-filled tube feet for

Below: A squid can move rapidly by using jet propulsion. The mantle cavity, a water-filled chamber on the underside of the animal, is normally open to the outside and so is full of water. By pressing the edge of the mantle against its funnel and squeezing the muscles of the mantle, the squid forces water out through the funnel and is propelled backward.

moving about, and a sea urchin walks on its spines.

Other animals swim. The protozoan *Paramecium* swims by using rows of tiny cilia like oars. A sea butterfly is a type of sea snail, and it uses a pair of "wings" to swim about. A squid has a pair of wing-like membranes along its sides that help it move. Waves passing along these membranes propel the squid gently forward through the water. A squid can also propel itself rapidly backward by forcing water out through a funnel-shaped hole under its head.

Fishes are among the best swimmers, most of which have streamlined bodies. Some of a fish's forward propulsion comes from waves of muscle contraction passing down the body, but most is provided by the side-to-side movement of the tail. The pectoral ("shoulder") fins are used for braking and steering.

Reptiles, birds and mammals are basically land animals, but some have become adapted for life in the water. Turtles use their paddle-like limbs for swimming, and penguins literally fly under water. Seals are superb swimmers; their limbs have become powerful flippers. Whales and dolphins propel themselves by horizontal tail fins, called flukes.

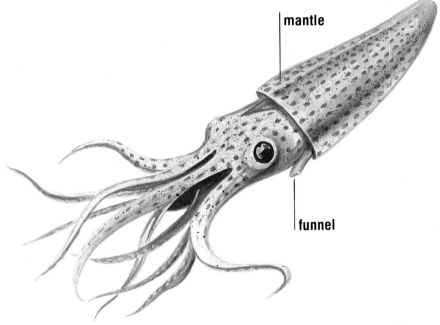

mantle

funnel

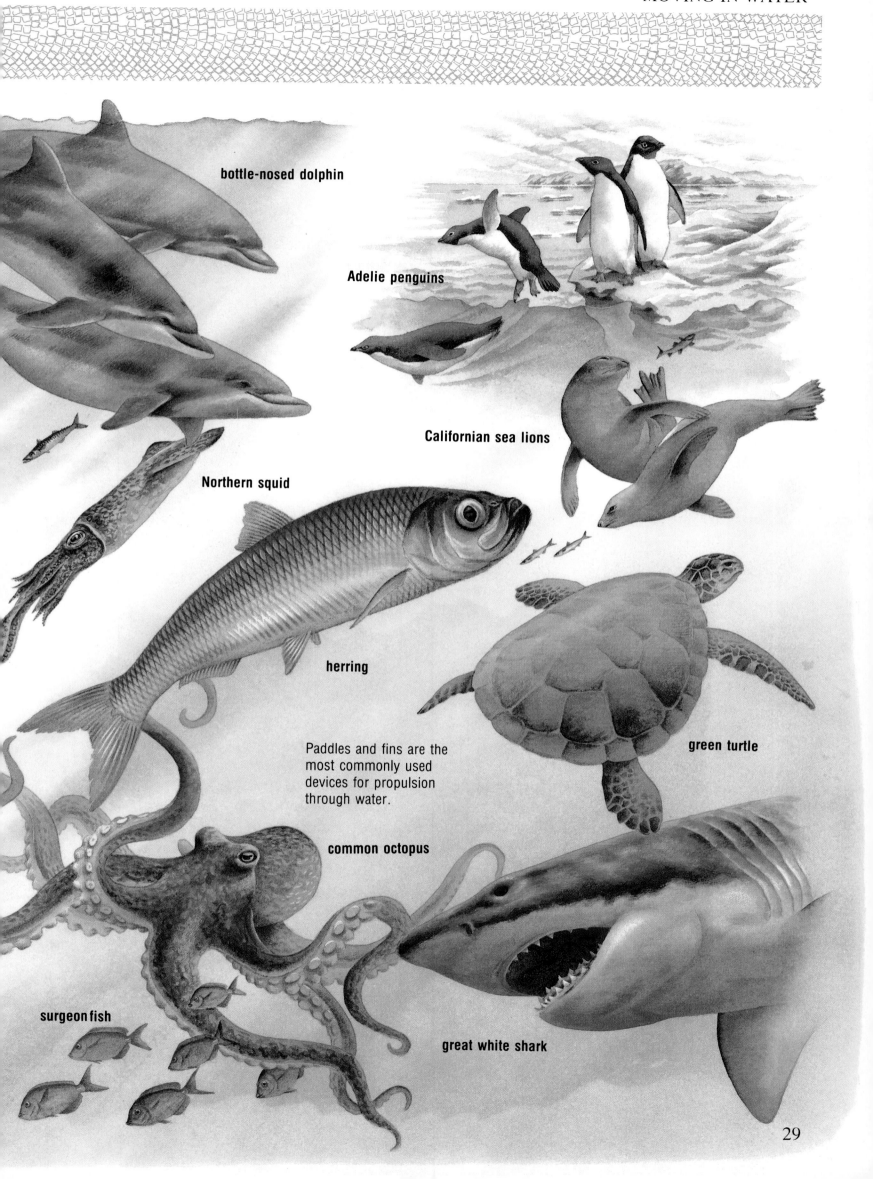

bottle-nosed dolphin

Adelie penguins

Californian sea lions

Northern squid

herring

Paddles and fins are the
most commonly used
devices for propulsion
through water.

green turtle

common octopus

surgeon fish

great white shark

MOVING ON LAND

Some land animals crawl about, keeping their bodies on the ground all the time. Snails and slugs, for example, move in the same way as their water-dwelling relatives (see page 28).

An earthworm also moves by causing waves of contraction to pass down its body. Each segment of the earthworm's body contracts in turn, and as it does, it becomes fatter and small bristles located on each side of the body grip the surrounding soil. Segments in front of the anchored point are extended and pushed forward through the soil. Segments behind are drawn up and then contracted.

Nearly all other land animals have legs, which enable the body to be raised off the ground. A millipede or centipede has many legs on each segment of its body. Waves of leg movement pass from front to back down the animal.

Insects have only six legs and can thus move faster. An insect is still very stable, however, because it has at least three legs on the ground all the time. In grasshoppers and fleas one pair of legs is modified for jumping; mantises use a pair of legs for holding prey.

Vertebrates have four limbs. In

Above: Like other lizards, a gecko holds its legs out sideways and tends to drag its belly along the ground. The pads on a gecko's feet are equipped with thousands of microscopic hooks. These enable it to cling onto apparently smooth surfaces, even glass.

a typical amphibian, such as a salamander, the legs are held out sideways from the body, so the animal's belly trails along the ground. Frogs and toads, on the other hand, have powerful hind legs for jumping and swimming.

Reptiles such as crocodiles, tortoises and lizards also walk with their legs held out sideways, but snakes have no legs. Usually when a snake moves, it throws its body into waves that push against stones and other things on the ground. Most snakes, however, can also move along slowly by using their belly scales. Sidewinding snakes are so named because they move sideways across sand rapidly in movements like steps.

Mammals typically walk on legs that are held underneath the body. This way the belly is kept clear of the ground and the mammal is able to move quicker. Mammals are less stable than reptiles, but keep their balance using special organs located in their ears.

In some mammals, such as an armadillo, the whole foot rests on the ground. A wolf, on the other hand, walks on its toes and can run more swiftly. Among the swiftest animals are those such as antelopes and horses, which run on hooves at the tips of their toes.

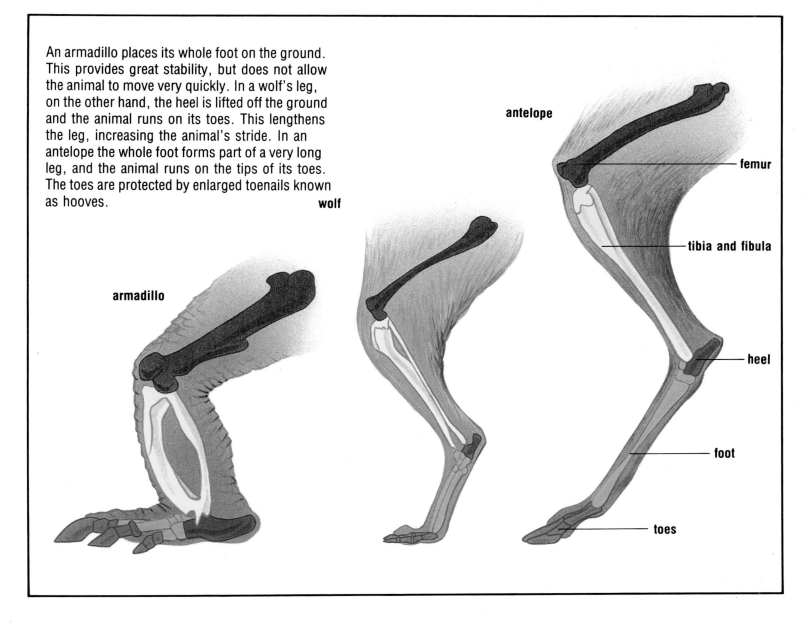

An armadillo places its whole foot on the ground. This provides great stability, but does not allow the animal to move very quickly. In a wolf's leg, on the other hand, the heel is lifted off the ground and the animal runs on its toes. This lengthens the leg, increasing the animal's stride. In an antelope the whole foot forms part of a very long leg, and the animal runs on the tips of its toes. The toes are protected by enlarged toenails known as hooves.

wolf

antelope

femur

tibia and fibula

heel

armadillo

foot

toes

FLIGHT

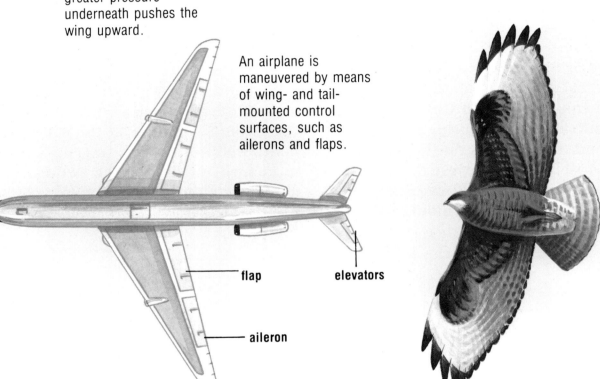

An airplane's wing generates lift by causing the air traveling over the top to move faster than the air underneath. The pressure of the air on top is reduced, and the greater pressure underneath pushes the wing upward.

An airplane is maneuvered by means of wing- and tail-mounted control surfaces, such as ailerons and flaps.

flap

elevators

aileron

A buzzard has large, broad wings designed to generate large amounts of lift at slow speeds. Control is achieved by altering the angle of the wings and movements of the feathers.

Birds, insects and bats have mastered flying, and keep themselves in the air by flapping their wings. All other flying animals, such as flying squirrels, flying possums, flying lemurs, flying lizards, flying frogs and flying fish, only glide through the air.

Flying involves creating two forces. One is lift, which pushes upward and overcomes the downward pull of gravity. The other force is thrust, which pushes forward and overcomes the backward force of drag created by air resistance. In an airplane, for example, lift is created by a specially shaped wing. Air travels faster over the upper surface and the air's pressure is reduced. The higher pressure underneath the wing pushes it upward. Thrust is created by the airplane's engines.

A bird's wing has a similar shape to that of an airplane, so lift is created the same way. Thrust is produced by the flapping wings; feathers at the wing tips twist as the wings move downward, and the twisting action produces a backward moving flow of air that drives the bird forward. Thrust is also created by the flexing of the feathers at the back of the wings.

The wings of birds vary in shape, according to where the birds live and how they fly. The wings of an albatross, for example, are long and thin, for gliding rapidly, using updrafts from the sea to keep it aloft. In contrast, a buzzard has broad wings for slow, soaring flight

An Alpine swift has thin swept-back wings for fast flight–like the wings of a jet fighter airplane.

The long, thin wings of an albatross enable it to glide near the surface of the sea as it searches for food.

The short, broad wings of a pheasant are designed so it can take off rapidly among trees when disturbed.

high in the air. A swift has fairly long, swept-back wings for high-speed flight. A pheasant has short broad wings to enable it to take off rapidly among trees.

Instead of feathered wings, bats have thin membranes, stretched between the front and hind limbs and supported by four long "fingers" of the front limb. The membrane curves to give the airfoil shape that produces lift. Thrust is generated by the flexing of the rear edge of the membrane.

Insects have flat wings. But being mostly very light, they still manage to flap their wings so that lift and thrust are produced.

Some insects are a puzzle. A bee, for example, is, in theory, too heavy to get off the ground!

Above: A bird generates lift and thrust by flapping its wings downward and forward.

Left: Bats are the only mammals capable of true flight. When flapped, the wings becomes curved, thus creating the necessary lift as it moves through the air. Thrust is produced at the trailing edge of the wings.

SENSES

Mammals are said to have five main senses—sight, hearing, taste, smell, and touch. Most of the main sense organs are located in the head, near the brain.

Animals need senses to locate food and to detect the presence of others. The five main senses are vision, hearing, taste, smell and touch, but animals do have other senses as well.

Many animals have organs sensitive to light. In the eye of a vertebrate, a lens focuses an image onto a layer of light-sensitive cells. An insect's eye consists of many tube-like units, each of which has a lens and light-sensitive cells.

Animals hear by sensors that detect sound vibrations. In insects and vertebrates, a membrane, called the tympanum – known in mammals as the ear-drum – picks up the vibrations and transfers them to sense cells.

Taste and smell are similar senses that involve the use of sense cells to detect chemicals. Taste cells in the mouth react to the presence of chemicals in food. An organ of smell detects airborne chemicals.

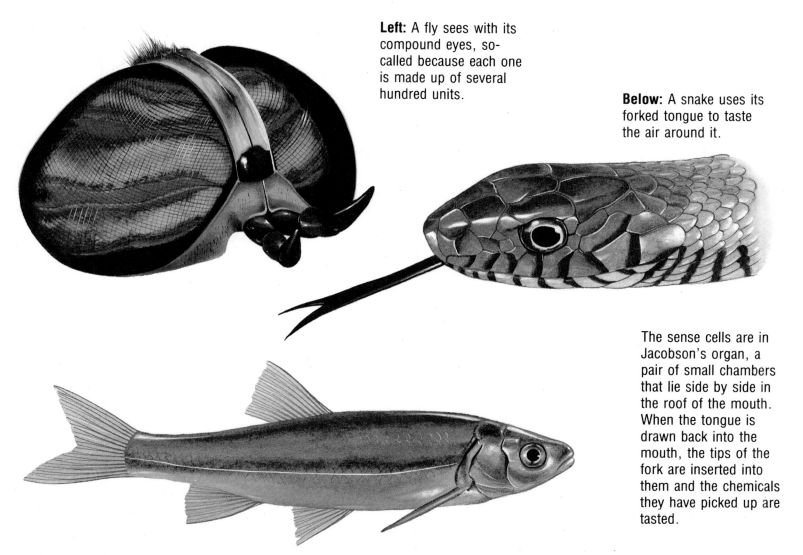

Left: A fly sees with its compound eyes, so-called because each one is made up of several hundred units.

Below: A snake uses its forked tongue to taste the air around it.

The sense cells are in Jacobson's organ, a pair of small chambers that lie side by side in the roof of the mouth. When the tongue is drawn back into the mouth, the tips of the fork are inserted into them and the chemicals they have picked up are tasted.

Above: A fish uses a special sense system. Called the lateral line system, this detects what is happening around the fish. The line along the side of the body is actually a canal just beneath the surface. The canal contains a row of pressure-sensitive organs.

Left: A scallop is equipped with two rows of eyes just inside the shell. These cannot detect shapes, but they are sensitive to changes in the amount of light. So when a shadow passes over the scallop, it is detected immediately and the scallop closes quickly.

The sense of touch is a complex sense. It involves more than one kind of sensor and can be considered as several different types of sense. In the skin of a human, for example, there are touch receptors, pressure receptors and pain receptors, as well as sensors that detect heat and cold. There are also sense organs called proprioceptors. These provide information about conditions inside the body, such as the degree to which a muscle is stretched and the position of the body in relation to the pull of gravity. All these combine to create a feeling when you move a part of the body.

Other senses animals have include those for detecting changes in temperature, changes in the humidity of air and changes in the salt content of water.

A fish has a sense system known as the lateral line system. This consists of a row of pressure sensors along each side of its body. These detect vibrations in the water around the fish. Sharks and some other fish also have organs in their faces that are sensitive to tiny electrical fields generated by other fish. A duck-billed platypus can detect the tiny electrical fields generated by shrimps.

COMMUNICATION

An animal may need to communicate with another for many reasons. It may wish to signal that it is ready to reproduce and is seeking a suitable mate. It may wish to warn off rivals. Or, it may be giving a warning to others that there is danger about.

Animals use a variety of visual, audible and chemical signals in order to communicate. Humans communicate basically by means of

sounds, which we have developed into a variety of languages that can be written down and conveyed visually. Human beings also communicate a great deal by means of other visual signals, such as using our hands and sometimes even our whole body to convey a specific message.

Many other animals are able to communicate by means of sound. Birds, for example, sing to

Above: A male frog croaks to attract a mate. The sound is produced by forcing air past two flaps of skin in the frog's throat. The species shown here is a painted reed frog.

Above right: A chimpanzee shows emotions by using facial expressions (from top): a look of thoughtfulness; a grin of pleasure; a "laugh" to show anger.

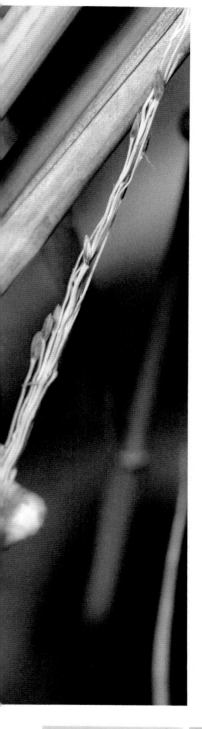

advertise their presence. Geese cackle loudly when danger threatens, but honk gently when flying in formation so they keep together. Grasshoppers signal by rubbing their hind legs against their wings; about 13 different signals are possible. Frogs croak to attract mates. Whales "sing" to each other over hundreds of miles.

Visual signals are even more common. Bright colors may be important in attracting potential mates, and many animals perform courtship displays (see page 54). The male fiddler crab, for example, uses its huge claw both for signaling to potential mates and for warning off rival males. A worker honey bee that has discovered a new source of food tells others in the nest about her find by means of an elaborate dance combined with sound signals. Chimpanzees, like humans, are able to convey messages by facial expressions.

Chemical signals are also important to many animals. Ants lay scent trails between nests and food sources so workers can journey to and fro without getting lost. Many mammals use scent to mark the borders of their territory. A female moth attracts males by releasing scent; male moths detect minute traces of this scent with their huge feathery antennae.

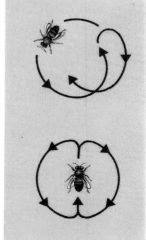

Left: When a worker bee finds a new source of nectar she returns to the hive and performs a waggle dance. This shows other workers the distance and direction. A nearby source is shown by a simple round dance. A more distant source is shown by a circle that is then divided in half. The angle of the dividing line tells the other bees the direction of the food in relation to the direction of the Sun.

INSTINCT AND LEARNING

Some of an animal's behavior is learned, acquired gradually as the animal grows up and discovers more about the world around it. Other forms of behavior are purely instinctive. This means they do not have to be learned. Instinctive behavior is inherited from an animal's parents. It is as much a part of the animal as other inherited features, such as the color of its fur, feathers or shell.

Instinctive behavior is often a form of protection. A young mammal, such as a kitten, for example, instinctively fears the edge of a sheer drop, even if the space is covered with a sheet of glass that the kitten can feel with its paw. The same instinctive fear of heights is often found in humans.

Most of the behavior found in invertebrates is instinctive, although some insects show a limited ability to learn. Higher animals, on the other hand, learn as they get older. In general, the more advanced the animal, the greater is its ability to learn. Many animals learn their way around their local area; even a turtle can learn to find its way through a simple maze. Young birds have to learn to land efficiently by facing into the wind. Rats and squirrels learn to solve quite complex problems to reach food sources.

In many cases, learned behavior

goose

hawk

A newborn chick is instinctively afraid of anything that moves. Gradually, however, it learns to tell the difference between predators (above) and harmless animals (left).

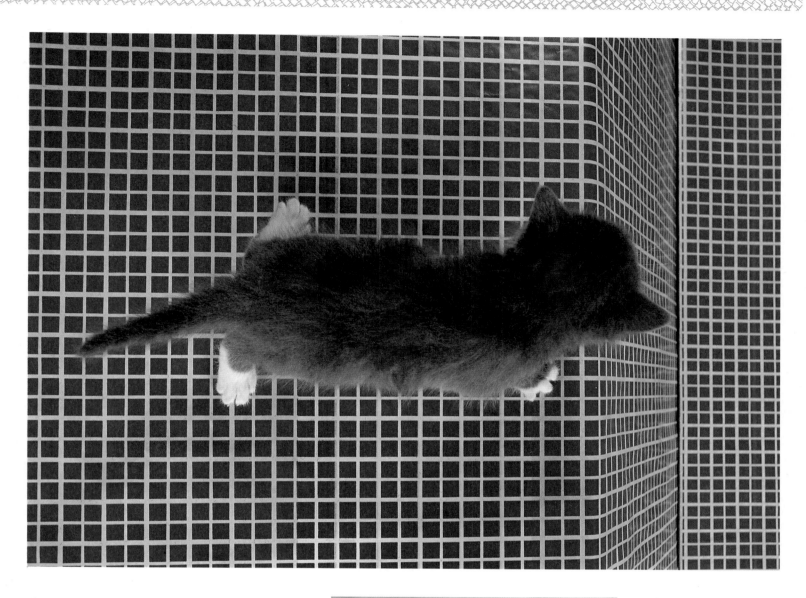

is defined as instinct modified by experience. This is illustrated by young carnivores which have an instinctive desire to chase things but still have to learn how to kill prey effectively to survive as adults. The instinctive reaction of young chicks to the appearance of objects above them is also modified by experience. Initially, chicks automatically cower and seek protective cover even if a leaf drifts overhead. After a while, however, chicks learn to tell the difference between harmless things and potential predators. They even learn the difference between ducks and geese, which have long necks, and birds of prey, which can be recognized by their short necks.

Above: A four-week-old kitten instinctively draws back from what appears to be a sheer drop, even though the space is actually covered by a transparent sheet of plastic or glass.

Left: A young carnivore, such as this lion cub, plays with anything that moves. In the process, the cub improves its hunting technique and learns what can and cannot be successfully attacked.

DESERT ANIMALS

Water makes up a large part of an animal's body, and replacing any lost water is vital to an animal's survival. In desert areas water is scarce, so desert animals have developed ways of conserving what little water there is available.

Most deserts are hot places and heat tends to increase water loss from an animal's body. Also, many vital body processes stop working if the body gets too hot, so it is essential that an animal keeps its body temperature down to a reasonable level. One way of doing this is to sweat; the evaporation of liquid from the body's surface helps cool the body. This however, involves losing precious water.

Many desert animals avoid the problems of heat and water loss by spending all day in burrows and only coming out to feed at night when it is cooler. Plant-eating animals conserve water by producing very dry feces and only small amounts of very concentrated urine. Some rodents store food in underground burrows, where the food absorbs moisture from the air. Another survival technique is that of the thick-tailed mouse of the Sahara Desert. This mouse stores fat in its tail that is converted into water when needed.

Larger desert animals must put up with the desert's heat. Camels and types of antelopes, such as oryx and addax, allow their bodies to heat up more than other animals, only starting to sweat at much higher temperatures than usual Addax never drink; they manage to survive on dew and the water in their food. Camels can go for long periods without drinking.

Predatory animals have fewer problems; their prey contains most of the water they need. Again, many of them rest during the day, becoming more active at night when rodents and other plant-eaters emerge from their burrows. The large ears of a desert fox, such as the fennec that lives in the Sahara Desert, are useful for locating prey. During the day, the large surface areas of the ears help the fox lose excess heat.

The sandgrouse is one of the few birds that live in deserts. It flies long distances to collect water in its breast feathers and transport the water back to its young.

desert rabbits store food in their burrows

Left: A sandgrouse may fly many miles to collect water for its chicks. The water is collected by soaking the breast feathers.

Small desert animals are most nocturnal (active at night). Larger species have evolved ways of coping with heat and drought.

oryx

camels store fat in their humps as reserves of energy

fennec

rattlesnake

kangaroo rat

thick-tailed gerbil stores fat in its tail

COLD CLIMATE ANIMALS

walrus

emperor penguin

seal

musk ox

Arctic fox

Arctic hare

Extreme cold can prevent body processes from being carried out as much as extreme heat (see page 40). Animals that need outside heat to warm their bodies, such as reptiles and amphibians, are not found in the coldest parts of the world. And the few kinds of insects that live in such places are generally found only during the warmer times of the year.

Mammals, on the other hand, are warm-blooded. This means they generate their own heat inside their bodies. Some mammals, therefore, are present at all times of the year even in the coldest parts of the world.

Some mammals avoid the harsh extremes of winter by hibernating (see page 44). Others, such as lemmings and voles, spend the winter in tunnels under the snow, away from the biting winds above. In mountain regions, pikas store hay in their burrows in order to provide themselves with enough food to survive the winter.

Animals that live above the ground have dense coverings of waterproof fur to keep them warm. Polar bears have white fur, and some animals, such as Arctic foxes and Arctic hares, are white in winter. This helps to camouflage them against the snow, and helps reduce heat loss, because white objects give out less heat than black or brown ones. Arctic animals also tend to have small ears and tails, to reduce the surface area of body exposed to the air.

In addition to fur, polar bears are insulated by a thick layer of fat, called blubber, just below the skin. They are the largest of all bears, and their sheer size also helps to keep them warm. Seals and penguins are also insulated with blubber. In the depth of the Antarctic winter, groups of Emperor penguins huddle together to keep each other warm.

Above: Animals of the Arctic and Antarctic are well insulated against the cold. White coloring helps to reduce heat loss and give camouflage.

Opposite: Emperor penguins breed during the Antarctic winter. Each young chick is kept warm by an adult.

Below: A polar bear is superbly adapted for life in the Arctic. The hairy soles of its feet enable it to walk on ice without slipping.

HIBERNATION

Many animals avoid the extremes of winter by going into hibernation. This is a form of deep, winter sleep, during which the animal is only just alive.

Before an animal goes into hibernation, it stores food reserves. If an animal cannot store enough food it may not survive the winter. Some animals, such as hamsters, store food in their burrows and wake up at intervals during the winter to feed. Other animals store their food reserves as body fat.

As an animal begins hibernation, its body temperature drops, and at the same time its body processes slow down. The heart beats more slowly and breathing may eventually become almost imperceptible. At times during the winter the animal's body temperature may be only a few degrees above freezing. This means the animal uses up the least possible amount of energy, which makes its food reserves last longer.

Animals that hibernate are found in all regions where winters are cold. In temperate regions, hibernators include hedgehogs, bats, dormice and several other kinds of rodent. Bears and raccoons sleep for long periods, but they are not true hibernators because they die if their body temperatures fall too low. Most mountain mammals, such as marmots, also hibernate. Arctic hibernators include the Arctic ground squirrel.

Some animals that live in regions prone to drought undergo a kind of summer "hibernation," called aestivation. Some desert rodents, for example, sleep through the hottest months of the year. African

and South American lungfishes also aestivate. As its stream starts to dry up, a lungfish creates a burrow in the mud. Inside the burrow the lungfish wraps itself in a cocoon, where it can survive for up to four years. It lives by absorbing some of its own muscle tissue. The water-holding frog of Australian deserts can remain in a sleep-like state in an underground burrow for several years between rainstorms.

Above: Like many other animals, a brown bear stores up fat during the summer and sleeps for most of the winter. This is not true hibernation, however, because the bear's temperature drops only a few degrees. The bear can wake up quickly if disturbed.

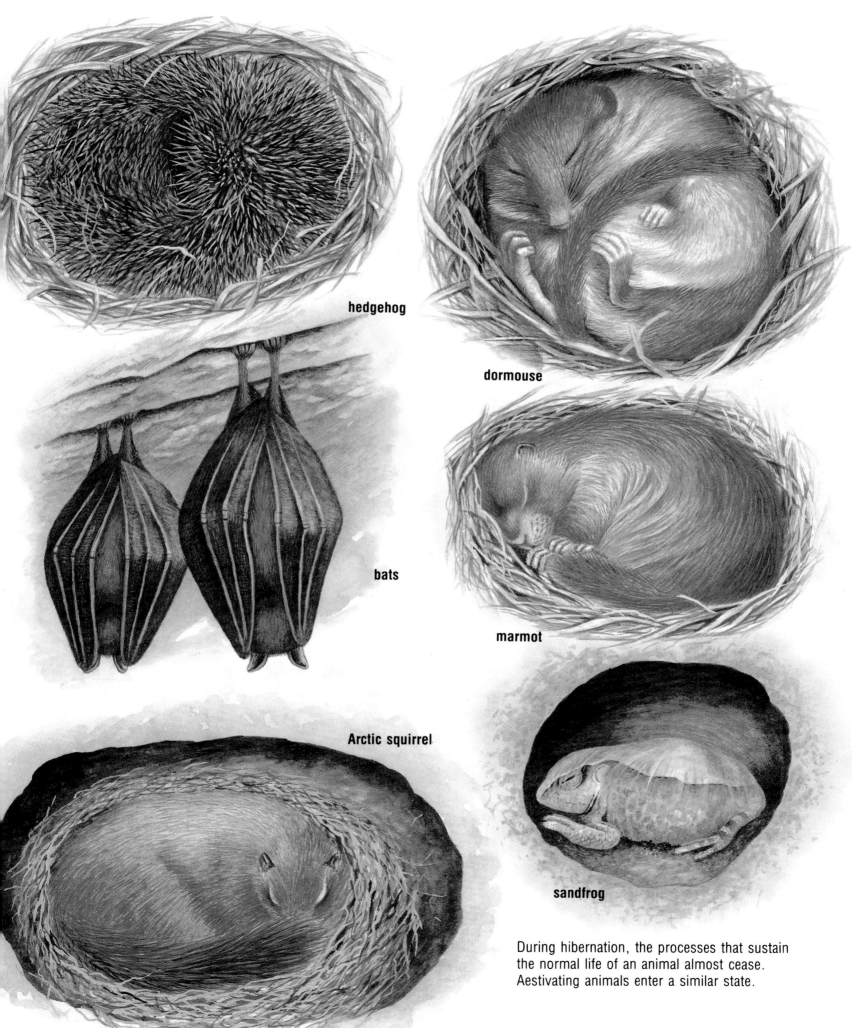

hedgehog

dormouse

bats

marmot

Arctic squirrel

sandfrog

During hibernation, the processes that sustain the normal life of an animal almost cease. Aestivating animals enter a similar state.

45

TOOL USERS

Humans tend to think of themselves as the only animals capable of using tools. But there are a number of other animals that have evolved the ability to use tools to obtain food, and in some cases as weapons.

A tool can be broadly defined as anything outside an animal's own body that the animal uses to help it achieve a purpose. A thrush, for example, uses a stone surface as an anvil on which to break open the shell of a snail for its food. An Egyptian vulture breaks open an ostrich egg by either smashing a stone against it or hurling the egg against a rock. A sea otter uses a stone like a hammer to break open the shells of clams.

One species of crab uses sea anemones as weapons. The crab holds two anemones, one in each pincer, and then waves them threateningly at an enemy. An archer fish uses water as a weapon. It squirts water at insects to knock them off leaves, into the water below where they can be eaten.

A female sandwasp digs a burrow in which she lays an egg and puts in a paralyzed caterpillar for the larva to feed on. She seals the top of the burrow with pebbles and soil, which she makes tight by using a small stone as a hammer. The Galapagos woodpecker finch uses a cactus spine held in its beak to pry beetle larvae out of dead wood for food. Bears sometimes throw objects in play or to discourage threatening animals. Some birds, such as the American green heron, use bait in order to help them fish.

But it is among the primates, the group of mammals to which

Animals that have evolved ways of using tools
include chimpanzees (left), sandwasps (below),
and sea otters (bottom); also the Galapagos
woodpecker finch (right) and the song thrush
(bottom right). The tools are what nature
provides — mostly sticks and stones.

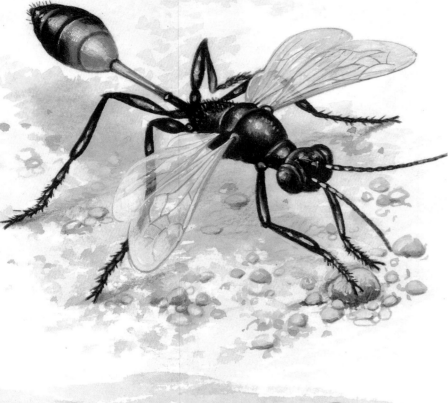

humans belong, that tool using has
evolved to the greatest extent.
Orangutans in zoos make swings
and ropes from cloth and straw.
Orangutans and chimpanzees
often join two sticks together to
make a longer one. Chimpanzees
also use twigs and sticks for prying
and levering. They even use leaves
to make sponges to soak up liquids.

47

ANIMAL HOMES

Some animals live, give birth and rear their young in the open. Others construct nests or dig burrows to live in.

Few invertebrate animals build homes, although some worms live in burrows and others construct tubes of stones or chalky material around themselves.

Among the vertebrates there are a few fishes, such as sticklebacks, that build nests. Some reptiles, such as alligators, do the same.

The best-known nest builders, however, are birds. Birds whose chicks hatch out blind, naked and helpless need to rear them under safe conditions, and a nest provides some protection against predators. Nests can vary from a crude

arrangement of plant material on the ground, to carefully constructed, cozy nests of mud, straw, moss and feathers in bushes and trees. Among the most elaborate nests are those of weaver birds. A male weaver bird weaves a hollow ball from grass and strips of leaf, leaving a single small entrance. Social weavers build huge communal nests that are used over and over again.

Other animals also make their homes in trees. Tree squirrels build nests using twigs, barks, leaves and mosses. These are called dreys. Orangutans often make temporary nests in which to spend the night, covering the nest with a shelter of leaves to keep out rain. Weaver

Above: Weaverbird nests hanging from the branches of a willow tree in South Africa. The occupants of these nests are safe from most predators.

field mouse

orangutan

weaver bird

Animals sometimes build homes for shelter, but more often to provide a cozy, safe place in order to rear their young.

badger

ants build nests of leaves by sticking the edges together with a sticky silk produced by larvae. Harvest mice build elaborate nests attached to the stems of grass and cereal stems.

Few animals build homes on the ground, as such homes are somewhat vulnerable to attack. The beaver does build at ground level, but its nest is protected by a water-filled pond, created by building a dam across a stream.

Other animals construct their homes by burrowing underground. A mole, for example, spends nearly all its life in the maze of tunnels it creates and maintains. Badgers, rabbits, rats, shrews, and wood mice are among the many animals that live in underground homes.

49

ANIMAL SOCIETIES

Some animals live largely alone, others live in families, and yet others live in large social groups. Each of these ways of life has its advantages and its disadvantages.

The main advantage of an animal's living independently is that a good supply of food is easier to guarantee. Many carnivorous mammals lead solitary lives, as predators often need large territories in which to hunt. But solitary animals can be found in most other animal groups, as well. Many solitary animals mark and defend territories, warning off intruders with aggressive behavior. The only social contact that such animals have is when a male and female come together to mate. And, in many cases, the pair behave aggressively toward each other when they first come in contact (page 54).

Sometimes animals live together in small groups. Often these are family groups, composed of an adult male, an adult female and one or more young. A family of wolves, for example, remains together for a year or two after the cubs are born. Wolves, like many other members of the dog family, are also pack animals. This means they hunt in groups of up to 25 individuals.

Lions also live in groups of up to about 20 individuals. Such a group is called a pride, and is made up of one or more adult males, a number of females and the young.

Some animals live in very large groups. The advantage is that in a group individuals are less likely to fall victim to predators. In many cases, some individuals act as sentries to warn the others if danger threatens. Animals that form

Bears live solitary lives. When two individuals meet, one may drive the other away. In contrast, rabbits live in large communities in which each individual is safer because of the presence of the others.

groups include primates, such as chimpanzees and most monkeys, and many kinds of birds and hooved, plant-eating mammals that graze in the open.

Smaller animals, such as rabbits, meerkats and prairie dogs, live in colonies in burrows. There is usually a strict social order in such groups, with some animals being dominant to others. Members of the same group, however, rarely fight each other. When two individuals come into conflict, the weaker usually just submits.

Right: Meerkats live in large social groups. They can often be seen standing on their hind legs to get a better view of what is around them. They seldom move far from their burrows, and at the first sign of trouble a bark from one individual alerts the whole group.

SOCIAL INSECTS

The most remarkable examples of social living are found among the social insects. Termites, ants, some kinds of wasps and some kinds of bees live in closely knit communities. In these communities, every individual works unselfishly for the good of the community as a whole. It is worth remembering, however, that this behavior is not thought out. It is purely instinctive and the insects involved cannot live in any other way.

Members of this type of community are of several different types, called castes. The central focus of the community is a single reproductive female, known as the queen. She founds the community and builds the beginnings of the nest. Once the community is established, however, laying eggs becomes the queen's only task.

A termite queen, for example, developes a huge, bloated body and becomes incapable of moving about. She lacks nothing, however, as she is carefully fed and tended by other members of the community. In a termite colony, the queen is generally accompanied by the king, a much smaller fertile male. The fertile males produced by ant, wasp, and bee communities, however, die soon after mating takes place.

The main tasks of building, cleaning, guarding the nest and providing food are carried out by the caste known as workers. In the nests of ants, bees, and wasps the workers are all infertile females, but termite workers are both sexes. In ant and termite colonies, some of the workers develop huge jaws or long snouts for squirting an irritating liquid. These are

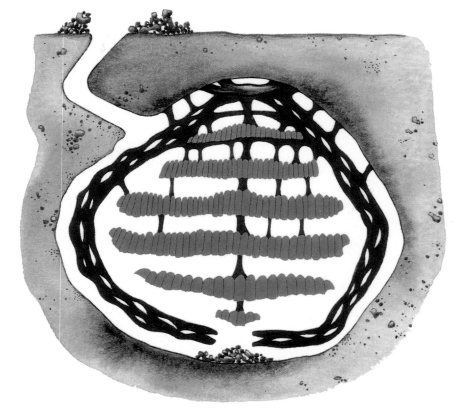

members of the soldier caste, who defend the nest.

Fertile males are generally produced in late summer, together with new queens. In a bee colony, the first queen to emerge kills the others and then flies off, followed by a swarm of males, called drones.

A wasp colony produces several new queens, which hibernate during the winter before founding new colonies in the spring. Ants and termites produce large numbers of flying males and females. After mating, the wings fall off and the fertilized females found new colonies.

Left: Huge termite mounds in Australia. Each mound may have about 2 million inhabitants, most of which are workers. The queen may live for up to 15 years, and some termite nests remain inhabited for up to 50 years.

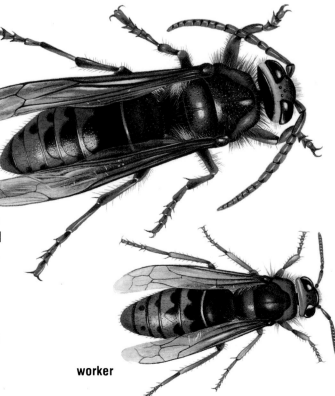

queen

worker

Far left: A wasp nest is often built in a hollowed out space underground. The queen begins the task of nest-building and rears the first larvae (center). These hatch out into workers, which are much smaller than the queen (right).

53

COURTSHIP

To produce offspring, a male and a female of the same species must mate. In many cases there is a period before mating during which one or both of the prospective mates perform certain rituals. This is called courtship.

Courtship has several purposes. First, it helps establish that the prospective mates are of the same species and of different sexes. This is particularly important where males and females are very similar in appearance. Courtship also establishes that the participants are ready to mate, and helps to overcome the natural aggression that usually keeps individuals apart as they compete for food.

Probably the most important purpose of courtship, however, is to ensure that healthy females mate with the strongest, most perfectly adapted males. In this way a species ensures that the best characteristics are passed on to the next generation. In many cases males vie with one another for the attention of females, and fights may occur. Males are seldom killed in such fights, but the dominance of the stronger males is established.

The length and degree of courtship varies considerably. When males have fought to establish dominance, mating often follows with little or no further courtship. A stag, for example, mates with the does in his harem with little ceremony. A male grayling butterfly, on the other hand, performs an elaborate courtship dance in front of his intended mate.

Above: Male and female albatrosses are alike and they display to each other during courtship.

In many courtship rituals males display to females. Black grouse (above) compete in display grounds, or leks, for the attention of females. A grayling butterfly (right) flutters around a potential mate, and a common newt (bottom) acquires a crest, black spots and an orange belly.

Sometimes males take on courtship colors, as in the case of the stickleback. A male common newt develops a distinctive crest and dark spots on his body. Garden snails circle around each other, getting closer and closer, before firing needle-like "love darts" into each other's skin, which stimulates the start of mating.

Elaborate courtship rituals are very common among birds. Male black grouse all perform together in an area known as the lek. The females choose the males that have produced the best displays. Male birds of paradise dance to show off their magnificent plumage. When the sexes are alike, both partners perform. Great crested grebes, for example, perform a complex series of dances before mating.

REPRODUCTION

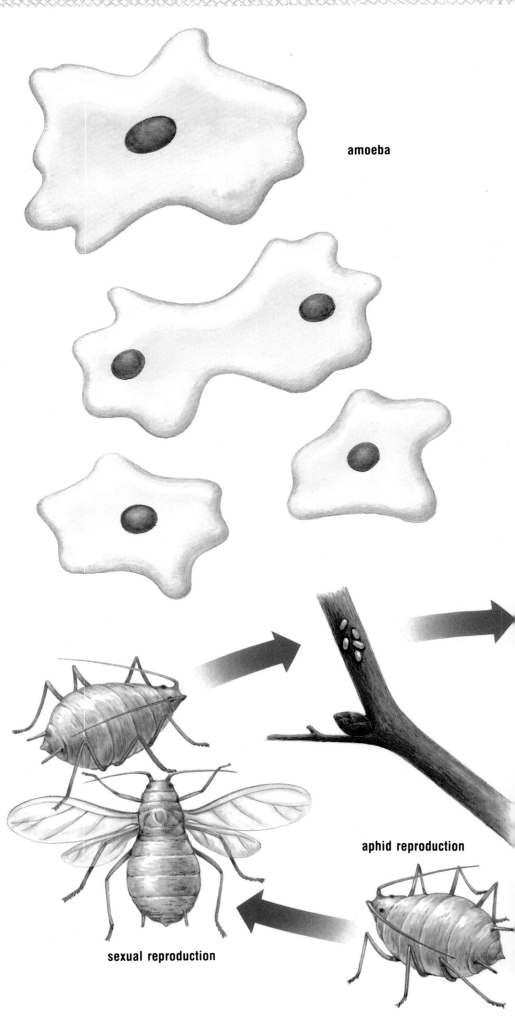

amoeba

aphid reproduction

sexual reproduction

All animals eventually die. But before they do they must try to reproduce themselves to ensure that the species continues. A single cell reproduces itself by dividing into two. Each new cell contains a new cell nucleus, a copy of the original one, and a set of organelles (see page 9). This process is the basis for all reproduction in the living world.

There are two forms of reproduction, asexual and sexual. Asexual reproduction requires only one parent and the offspring are all identical to the parent. An amoeba, for example, reproduces by simply dividing into two, a process that happens again and again. A hydra, a type of freshwater coelenterate, reproduces by budding a group of cells on its side that develops into a new individual. It eventually drops off and lives independently.

Large numbers of new individuals can be produced by asexual reproduction, and many animals that reproduce sexually have an asexual stage during their lives. Aphids, for example, reproduce asexually during the summer by a process called parthenogenesis. During this process, unfertilized egg cells develop into new individuals. Asexual reproduction enables an animal population to increase rapidly when food is abundant.

An amoeba reproduces itself simply by dividing into two (above right). The nucleus divides first, followed by the rest of the cell. The reproduction of other animals is generally a sexual process, in which a female egg cell is fertilized by a male sex cell (far right). Some animals can reproduce both sexually and asexually.

During sexual reproduction two individuals each contribute one special sex cell. In most cases the female sex cell is larger and is known as the egg, or ovum. The male sex cell, a sperm, is smaller and capable of swimming to the female sex cell. The two cells fuse in a process called fertilization. The resulting cell eventually develops into a new offspring.

In sexual reproduction each parent contributes half the genetic material. This results in different combinations of the characteristics of the parents. Variety among the offspring is increased because the genetic material is sometimes broken up and recombined during the production of sex cells. This variety helps species adapt and evolve. (See Evolution on page 16.)

Above: A Roman snail lays its eggs in the soil. The eggs have already been fertilized with spermatozoa from another snail.

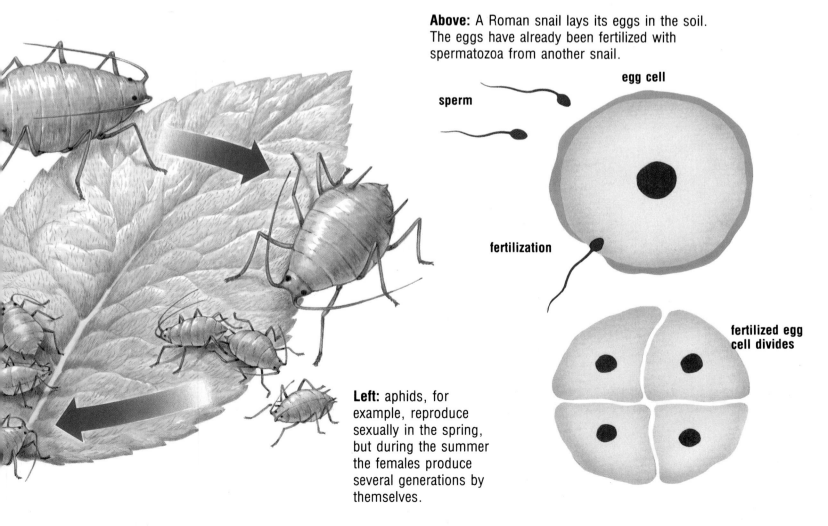

Left: aphids, for example, reproduce sexually in the spring, but during the summer the females produce several generations by themselves.

sperm

egg cell

fertilization

fertilized egg cell divides

RAISING YOUNG

After an egg has been fertilized, it starts to develop into a young animal. Part of the egg forms the yolk, which is used to feed the developing young. When there is very little yolk, as with most invertebrates, the young hatches out from the egg relatively soon. In many cases the young that emerges is a larva quite unlike the adult. The purpose of the larva is to feed and grow until it becomes an adult. It cannot reproduce and all its energy goes into increasing its size. When it is large enough, it changes into an adult.

Reptiles and birds produce larger eggs with more yolk. Thus their offspring remain inside for longer and hatch out at a more advanced stage of development. Mammals, however, retain their developing

A female scorpion carries her young around on her back until after their first molt. This increases their chance of surviving to become adults.

dingo and pup

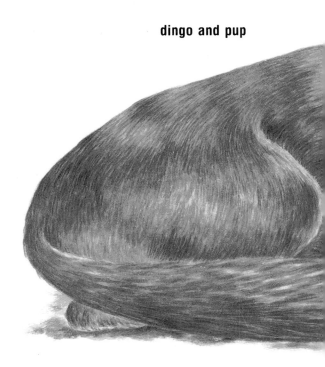

All mammals and birds look after their young. Cichlid fishes, on the other hand, are unusual among fishes, most of which abandon their eggs as soon as they are produced.

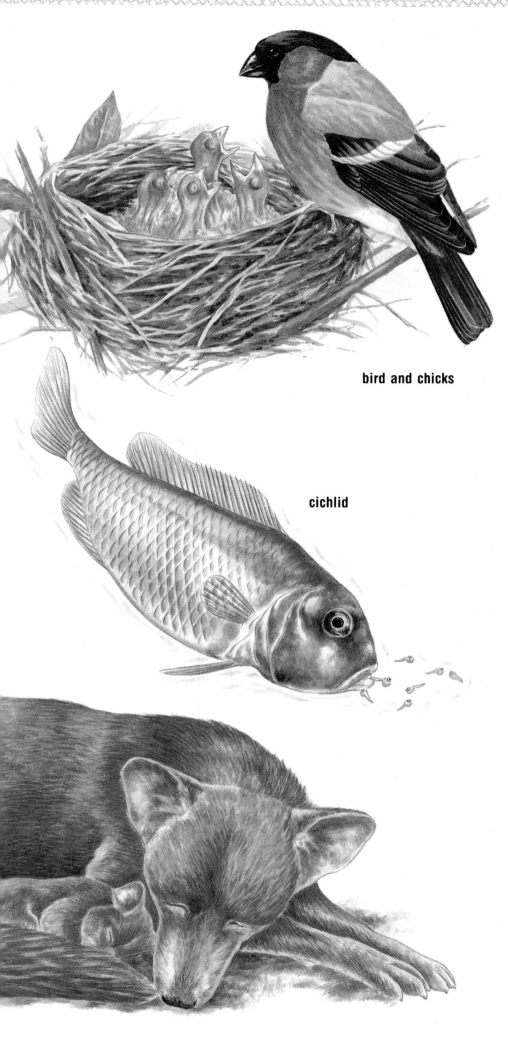

bird and chicks

cichlid

young inside their bodies and keep them nourished through an organ called a placenta.

The degree to which animals look after their young has a direct bearing upon how many young are produced. Species that take no steps to protect or look after their developing offspring have to produce huge numbers to make sure that just a few survive. Many butterfly larvae, for example, fall prey to birds. Tons of crab larvae are eaten by sea animals, and the eggs, called spawn, and tadpole larvae of frogs provide food for freshwater creatures.

Animals that take some care of their developing young produce fewer offspring. In general, therefore, reptiles produce fewer eggs than amphibians and fish. Birds, all of which look after their young after they hatch, produce even fewer eggs. And many mammals, when the young are cared for by one or both parents for some time after they are born, produce as few as one or two offspring at a time.

There are, however, some instances of parental care in other animal groups. Many spiders carry their eggs around with them and stand guard over the young after they hatch. Cichlid fishes do the same, and some cichlid parents take their tiny offspring into their mouths to protect them when danger threatens. A female Surinam toad carries her developing young embedded in her back until they have developed into tiny adults. Several lizards and snakes keep their eggs inside them until they hatch, thus producing active young.

LIFE CYCLES AND LARVAE

The eggs of many animals develop into larvae. Larvae are particularly common among animals that live in the sea, as swimming larvae are a useful way of spreading animal species over wider areas. The larvae of marine worms, crabs, shellfish, echinoderms and many others swim in a floating mass of tiny animals and plants called plankton.

But probably the most familiar larvae are those of insects, such as caterpillars, which become butterflies and moths, grubs, which become bees and beetles, and maggots which become flies. These larvae are simply feeding machines. They devour food, and at intervals they molt. This means they shed their relatively soft skins to make room for their rapidly growing bodies. After each molt a new, larger skin is revealed underneath.

After the final molt, however, the larvae undergo a complete change of form. This is called metamorphosis. The animal's head and legs disappear and the new skin is completely different. To begin with it is soft, but it soon hardens and darkens; the larva has become a pupa.

Nothing appears to happen for a time, but inside the pupa dramatic changes are taking place. The larva's body breaks down into a sort of nutritious "soup." A few small groups of cells remain and these develop into a new body. Finally, the animal emerges from the pupa in its adult form.

Other insects go through a more gradual metamorphosis. Grasshoppers, termites and dragonflies hatch out from their eggs as nymphs. Nymphs resemble the adults, but they have no wings and cannot reproduce. Like caterpillars, nymphs grow and shed their skins at intervals but there is no pupal stage. Nymphs just become adults, complete with wings, at the final molt. The tadpole of an amphibian goes through a similar gradual metamorphosis to become an adult newt, salamander, toad or frog.

Below: A newly-hatched tadpole takes in oxygen by means of external gills. These are soon replaced by internal gills and finally lungs. Meanwhile, the tadpole develops legs and finally loses its tail, so becoming a frog.

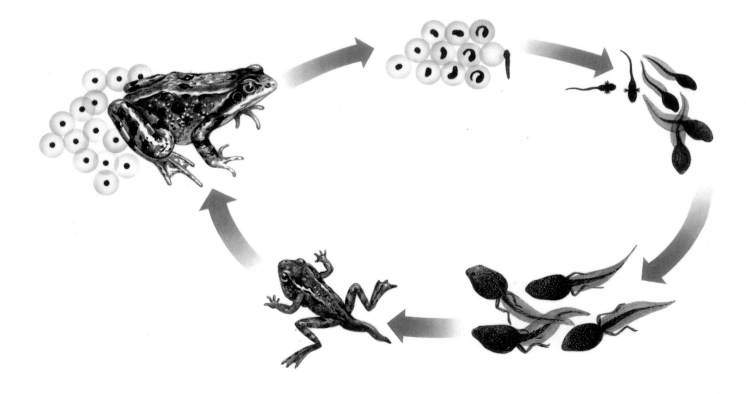

The life cycle of the monarch butterfly, populations of which are found in North and South America. The markings of the butterflies and their caterpillars warn potential predators that they are unpleasant to eat.

Male and female monarch butterflies mate tail to tail.

Inside the pupa, the caterpillar changes into an adult butterfly. Eventually the pupal case breaks open and the adult emerges.

After mating, the female butterfly lays a number of tiny eggs on the leaves of a plant that will provide food for the caterpillars. This is an egg belonging to a red admiral butterfly.

When it is fully grown the monarch caterpillar sheds its last caterpillar skin to reveal the shiny case of the pupa.

After it hatches, a monarch caterpillar feeds on various plants belonging to the milkweed family. These plants contain poisons that the caterpillar incorporates into its own blood.

MIGRATION

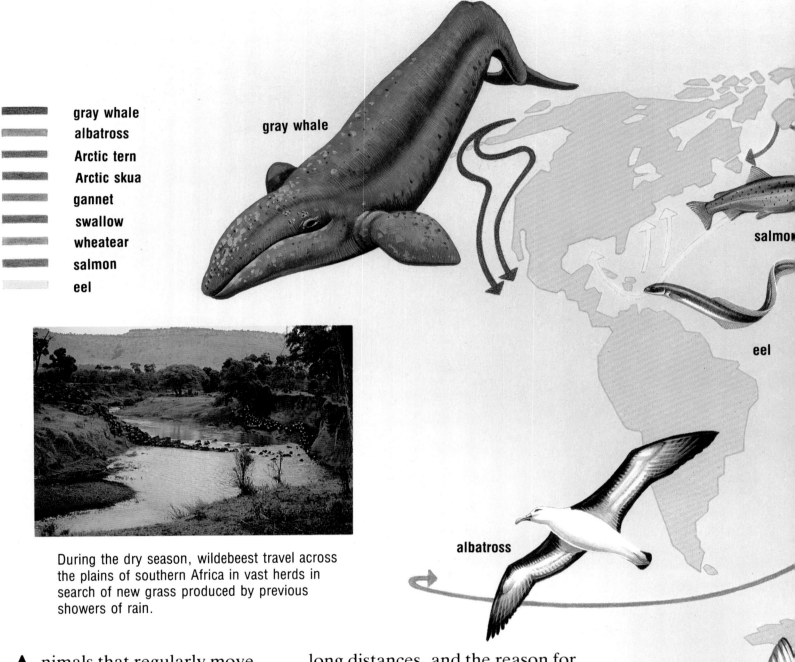

gray whale
albatross
Arctic tern
Arctic skua
gannet
swallow
wheatear
salmon
eel

gray whale

salmon

eel

albatross

Arctic tern

During the dry season, wildebeest travel across the plains of southern Africa in vast herds in search of new grass produced by previous showers of rain.

Animals that regularly move from one place to another are said to migrate. Generally, animals migrate to places where food is plentiful at a particular time of year. Many insect-eating birds that breed during the summer in temperate parts of the world, for example, move nearer the equator in the autumn, as few insects are around in temperate regions during the winter. In the spring, the birds fly back again as less food becomes available in the drier regions. Some northern birds migrate over very long distances, and the reason for this probably dates from the end of the last Ice Age about 11,000 years ago. As the ice retreated northward, insects colonized the newly exposed areas of land and the migrating birds followed them. But in the autumn, the birds continued to return to the winter feeding areas they had always used. Gradually, their autumn and spring journeys became longer and longer.

Food supplies are the cause of many migrations. The short-tailed shearwater follows shoals of fish

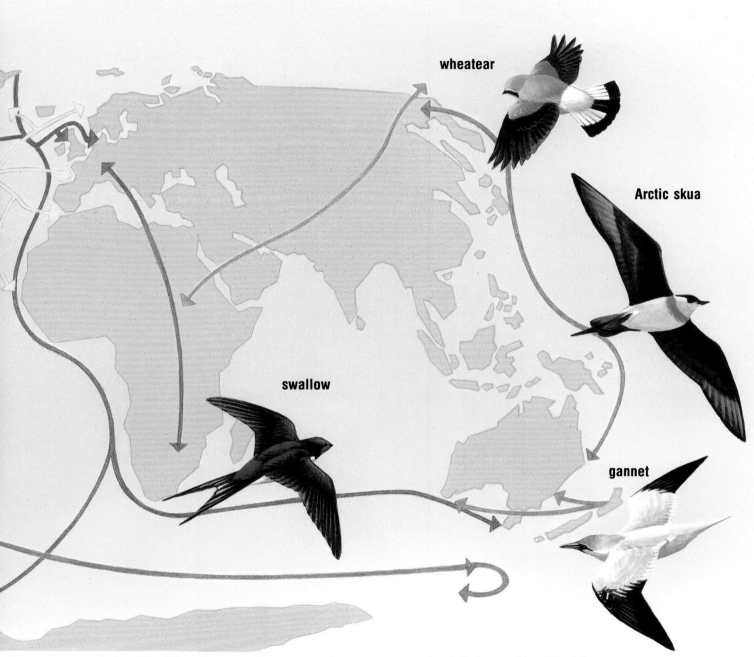

around the Pacific Ocean, but always returns to its breeding grounds on the shores of southern Australia. Herds of wildebeest, zebra and gazelle, migrate around the plains of East Africa, following the rains that make the grass grow. As summer begins, blue whales migrate from breeding grounds in tropical regions to polar waters rich in plankton. In North America, colonies of monarch butterflies move southward in the autumn, returning north in the spring.

Migrations are also often connected with breeding habits. Some animals migrate to a specific region or place to breed. Spiny lobsters, for example, feed in shallow waters but migrate over long distances in long single-file columns into deep water to breed. Eels migrate from the rivers of Europe and North America to the Sargasso Sea. Salmon swim from the sea up rivers to the streams in which they themselves hatched when they are ready to breed. Turtles may migrate thousands of miles to lay their eggs.

Migrating animals, particularly birds, fish and whales, often travel thousands of miles.

CAMOUFLAGE

Many animals have to hide to survive, and one way of hiding is to use colors and shapes to blend in with the surroundings. This way they avoid being seen by predators. Also camouflaged predators can get closer to potential prey without being noticed.

Greens and browns are the most common colors in nature, and thus these are the colors most often used by animals that need camouflage. A green tree frog, for example, may be hard to see against the green of a tropical plant. The sandy colored fur of a lion allows it to lie hidden in the dry grass of the African savannah. Other colors are useful. A brightly colored crab spider, for example, can remain hidden in a flower as it lies in wait for prey.

In many cases, the colors of animals are not uniform. Patterned colors help animals blend in with a patterned background, and often serve to break up the outline of an animal, making it even harder to see. Many moths and butterflies, for example, have mottled wings that enable them to rest on bark without being seen. The stripes of a tiger make it hard to see in the tall shady grass of the Asian jungle. A zebra's stripes perform a similar function and make it hard for a predator to pick out an individual in a moving herd.

Some animals go a step further and actually have irregular body

Right: This katydid from the rainforests of Costa Rica is easy to mistake for one of the leaves around it.

Animals use stripes, colors and shapes to camouflage or disguise themselves. This way, they may remain undetected by predators or potential prey.

crab spider

tiger

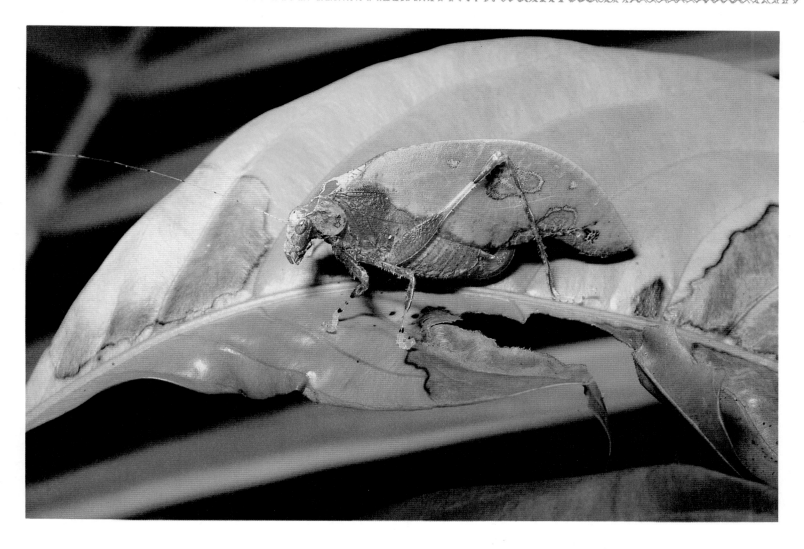

swallowtail moth caterpillar

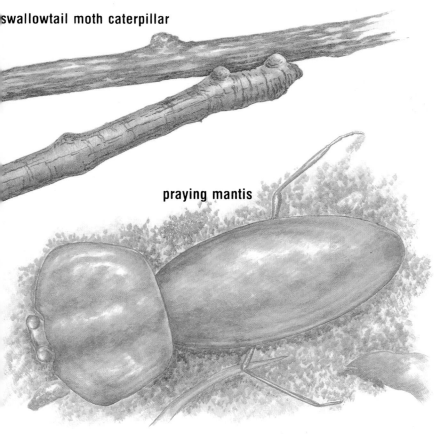

praying mantis

shapes to act as camouflage. The sargassum fish, for example, has weed-like projections that make it almost indistinguishable from the seaweed in which it hides.

Perhaps the most effective form of camouflage is to adopt a disguise. Stick insects resemble twigs or pieces of dead grass. Some caterpillars look like short twigs. At rest, such a caterpillar sticks out at an angle from a branch just like a real twig. Other caterpillars curl up on leaves to disguise themselves as bird droppings so passing birds ignore them. Thorn tree hoppers look like the thorns of a bramble. Other insects have the appearance of leaves, complete with "chewed" edges and brown, "diseased" patches, that help them complete their camouflage.

WARNINGS AND BLUFFS

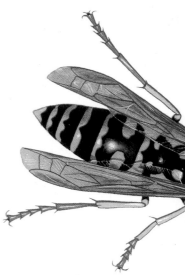

Left: Poison dart frogs, or poison arrow frogs, produce a poisonous substance in their skins. Their bright colors (red, orange, yellow, blue and black are used) indicate this fact to potential predators. The poison is used by the natives of South American rainforests on the darts and arrows with which they hunt the forest animals.

paper wasp

Left: When this eyed silkmoth suddenly exposes its huge "eyes", an attacker is, for a few moments at least, startled into believing it has attacked a much larger animal. By the time the attacker realizes its mistake, the moth has had a chance to escape.

Animals that defend themselves with poisons often use colors and patterns as a warning to deter predators. In many cases, poisons do not actually kill. Instead, they may merely taste very unpleasant or make the predator feel ill. Such animals advertise that they are poisonous with bright colors, so predators will leave them alone. A bird that has tried eating one or two cinnabar moths, for example, soon learns to associate their red markings with a nasty taste, and leaves other cinnabar moths alone.

Other animals with warning colors include the garden tiger moth, the monarch butterfly, the European fire salamander and the several kinds of arrow poison frogs of South America. A skunk's black and white markings are there to remind predators that this animal can squirt a truly horrible liquid into an attacker's eyes. The black and yellow markings of a wasp remind us all to avoid this insect's sting. Several other poisonous animals, including the caterpillar of the cinnabar moth, also have

Above: Animals use colors and markings to warn, startle or confuse predators. In some cases warnings are genuine–the markings of a wasp warn of its sting, those of an adder remind other animals of its bite. The markings of a puss moth caterpillar, on the other hand, are largely intended to scare an attacker. The caterpillar rears up, reveals its red collar and false eyes, and waves its two tails

false coral snake

adder

puss moth caterpillar

emperor moth

threateningly. As a last resort, it squirts formic acid. The markings of a false coral snake are pure bluff. The snake is harmless but predators often confuse it with a true coral snake, which is poisonous. The eye spots on the wings of the equally harmless emperor moth are designed to startle predators so that the moth has time to escape.

black and yellow markings, which help to reinforce their effectiveness as a warning.

Some non-poisonous animals cheat and take advantage of the warning colors used by poisonous ones. Hoverflies, for example, have black and yellow markings, and although the Hoverflies are harmless, birds tend to avoid them.

Harmless animals that mimic, or copy, the colors of poisonous ones are indulging in a form of bluff. Others have other ways of bluffing their way out of trouble. Some

butterflies, moths, and mantises have eyespots that can be exposed suddenly. A predator may be startled into thinking it has attacked a much larger animal. By the time the predator realizes its mistake, the insect has had a chance to escape. A few animals have false heads. A hair streak butterfly appears to have an eye and an antenna on the hind part of its wings. An attacker aims at what appears to be the head, but loses its meal as the butterfly takes off in the "wrong" direction.

ANIMAL PARTNERS

All animals live in communities with others. In most cases, members of a community live their lives fairly independent of one another. But some animals form partnerships in which two or more animals rely upon one another to help them survive.

The degree to which an animal relies on such a partnership varies. At one extreme are parasitic relationships, in which only one partner benefits and the other may actually be harmed (see page 70). At the other extreme are partnerships in which one partner may hardly be aware of the presence of the other. Some mites, for example, are hitchhikers. They attach themselves to the bodies of birds or insects and are carried to new sources of food, without affecting the host. A remora often travels by attaching itself by the sucker on its head to a shark.

Some hitchhikers are more beneficial to their hosts, and a partnership in which both partners benefit is know as a symbiotic association. Cattle egrets ride on the backs of antelope and warn them of approaching predators. Oxpeckers feed by removing the skin parasites of antelope and other savannah plant eaters. Sea anemones often ride on the shells of hermit crabs, placed there by the crabs themselves. In this symbiotic association the crabs seem to benefit by getting extra protection and the anemones probably get a better supply of food.

Sea anemones are found in other symbiotic relationships, as well. A clown fish, for example, is often among a sea anemone's tentacles. Cleaner fish and cleaner shrimps

Relationships between animals that benefit both partners are quite common. Cleaner fish, cleaner shrimps, and oxpeckers remove parasites from their hosts and obtain food in doing so. Hermit crabs often carry sea anemones around on their shells and clown fish often form associations with sea anemones.

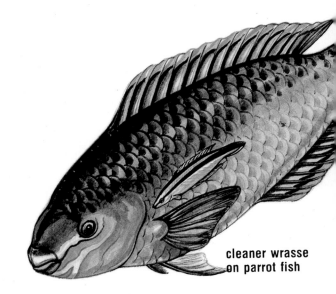

cleaner wrasse on parrot fish

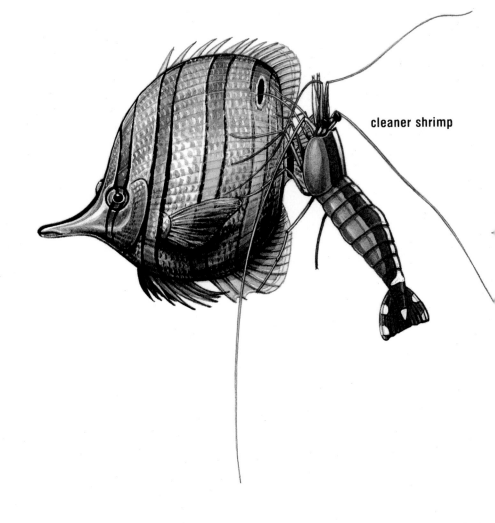

cleaner shrimp

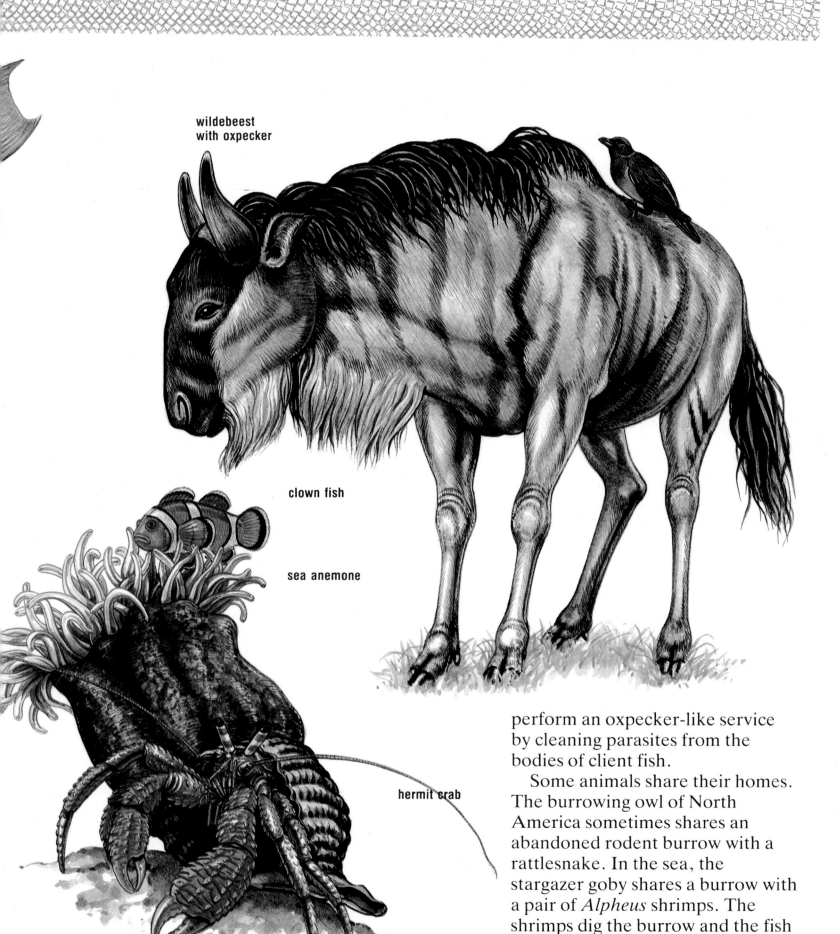

wildebeest
with oxpecker

clown fish

sea anemone

hermit crab

perform an oxpecker-like service by cleaning parasites from the bodies of client fish.

Some animals share their homes. The burrowing owl of North America sometimes shares an abandoned rodent burrow with a rattlesnake. In the sea, the stargazer goby shares a burrow with a pair of *Alpheus* shrimps. The shrimps dig the burrow and the fish therefore benefits by getting a home. The shrimps, which have rather poor sight, get early warning of approaching predators as they feed just outside the burrow.

ANIMAL PARASITES

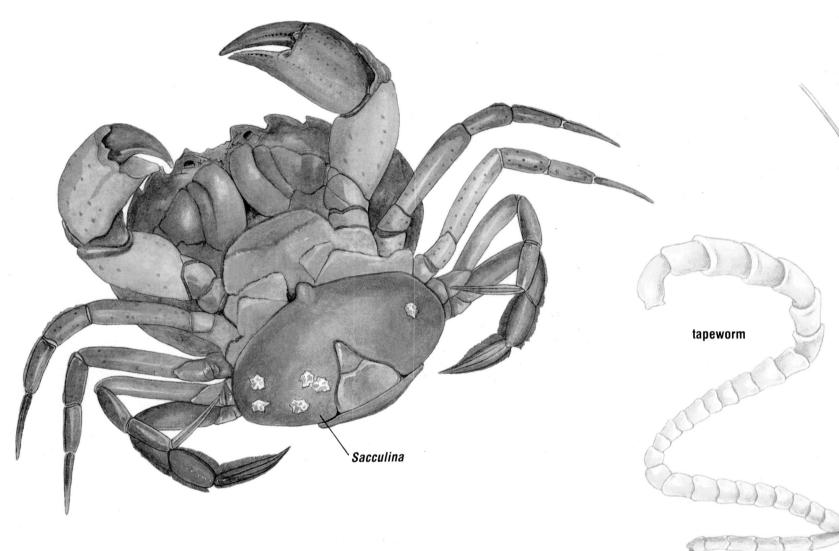

tapeworm

Sacculina

Some animals feed on plants, and some feed on other animals. Yet other animals have taken this a stage further, and remain more or less permanently in or on the bodies of the animals that provide them with their food. Such animals are called parasites.

Parasitism is a one-sided partnership, in which the parasite gets all the benefits. The other partner, called the host, gains nothing from the association, and may well be harmed. Many parasites eventually kill their hosts.

Almost all parasites are invertebrates, and their hosts are usually vertebrates. Parasitic protozoans, for example, include the parasite that causes malaria, *Plasmodium*. It is transmitted from one human to another by mosquitos.

The flatworm group is mostly composed of parasites, including tapeworms and several kinds of flukes. Most roundworms are free-living, but some are parasites of plants and others live off animals. River blindness and elephantiasis in humans are diseases caused by roundworms. All the above examples are endoparasites. That means they live inside the bodies of their hosts.

The annelid group of parasites, however, contains the leeches, which attach themselves to the outsides of their hosts and suck their blood.

Parasites are also found among the arthropods. The arachnids (spiders and their relatives) include

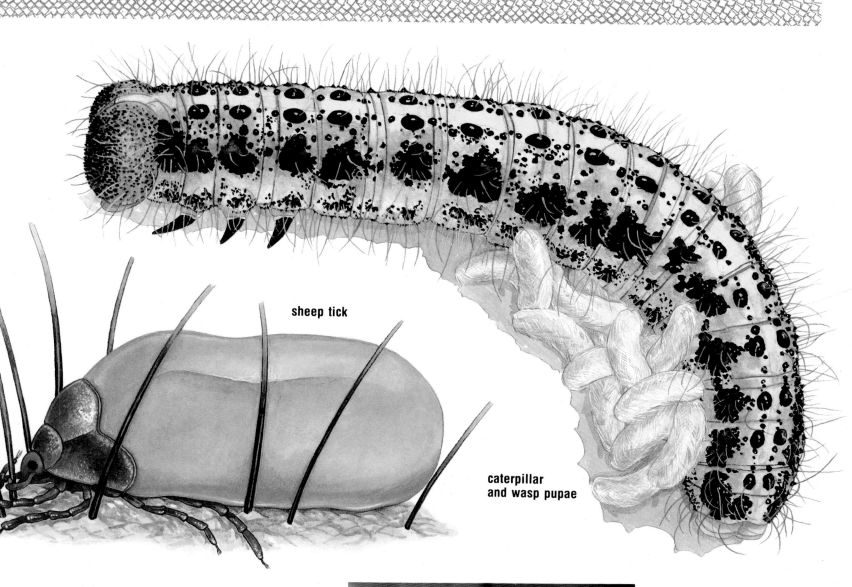

sheep tick

caterpillar
and wasp pupae

the blood-sucking ticks and a number of parasitic mites. Some crustaceans are also parasites, such as the fish lice. Parasitic copepods (another group of crustaceans) attack fish, worms and mollusks. The parasite *Sacculina*, a relative of barnacles, is a parasite on crabs. Parasitic insects include fleas.

Lampreys are the only true parasites among the vertebrates. They attach themselves to the bodies of fish and use their rings of hooked teeth to scrape away the flesh.

There are also about 100 kinds of birds that lay their eggs in the nests of other species and have the offspring raised by the host parents. Such birds are called brood parasites; the cuckoo is a well-known example.

Sacculina is a parasite of crabs. The parasite invades the crab's whole body, and eventually an orange mass, concerned with producing larvae, forms on the underside of the crab. Tapeworms are also internal parasites. Each mature segment contains ripe eggs, which when ejected with the host's dung may then infect other hosts. Ticks are external parasites that live on blood; the one shown here attacks sheep. The caterpillar shown here is carrying the pupae of a parasitic wasp. The caterpillar will soon die.

Left: A young cuckoo being fed by a white wagtail.

71

VANISHING WILDLIFE

The natural world is under threat. As the world's human population increases, more and more space is constantly needed to feed and house people. At the same time humans often exploit natural resources – even when such resources are not really needed – and the way humans produce food and process materials often causes harmful pollution.

As a result of such human activities much of the world's wildlife is disappearing. Many species are now extinct. That means they no longer exist. Many other species are currently under threat of extinction as a result of human actions.

In some cases, the threat of extinction is the result of over exploitation. On Mauritius, an island in the Indian Ocean, for example, there used to be thousands of the large birds called dodos. But during the seventeenth century the dodos were all killed by sailors in search of food. The dodos are now extinct.

Other animals have been hunted and some made extinct simply for their skins, shells or other trophies. Several kinds of rhinoceros, for example, are now endangered

Below: Sea turtles are now among the most endangered species for several reasons. They are hunted in large numbers for food and for their shells. Hunters also find and dig up sea turtles' nests. At the same time, their nesting beaches are increasingly damaged by tourist development. This species is known as the olive ridley sea turtle, which is found in both the Atlantic and Pacific oceans.

because humans have hunted them for their horns. Whales, deer, otters, and sea turtles have been greatly reduced in numbers because of overhunting.

Other animals have been displaced by species introduced into their habitats. Island animals are particularly vulnerable, because introduced animals such as goats, pigs, and deer may take over the supplies of food. Predators, such as cats, dogs and rats, have often been introduced by human carelessness. In many cases, the predators have caused native species to become extinct.

The most important reason why many of the world's animals are vanishing, however, is that their habitats are being destroyed. In some cases environments are damaged in the process of exploiting resources. In other cases, natural environments are altered to provide yet more land for farming. The world's rainforests, for example, are being destroyed at an alarming rate to provide timber and land for growing crops and raising cattle.

Other environments, particularly in the seas, are being affected by pollution; parts of the Mediterranean Sea are almost lifeless. As natural environments disappear, so, too, do the animals that live there.

Below: Animals are threatened by a number of factors, including pollution and overexploitation. Yet the biggest single cause of animals becoming endangered is the destruction of their natural habitats.

CONSERVATION

There are several important reasons for trying to conserve what remains of the world's wildlife. Fortunately, many people recognize this and are actively involved in conservation.

Plants are essential to the world. Only they can provide the food needed for animals, and ultimately humans. Plants are also vital in the processes that keeps the atmosphere replenished with oxygen.

Plants cannot survive by themselves. They merely form part of balanced communities of which animals are an essential part. At the same time, plants and animals form a potentially inexhaustible natural supply of materials and chemicals that can be of direct use

to humans. Thus, if humans do not succeed in conserving the world's natural communities of animals and plants, the result could be disastrous for humans.

Organizations concerned with wildlife conservation are at work in most parts of the world, particularly where wildlife is most under threat. The best-known international organizations are the International Union for the Conservation of Nature and Natural Resources (IUCN) and the Worldwide Fund for Nature (WWF). Some projects are concerned with trying to look after individual species, but increasingly people have come to realize that wildlife can only survive if environments are protected. In

Above: Most of the large whales are thought to be endangered, and steps are being taken to ensure their survival. Here, conservation scientists are releasing a humpback whale that has become entrapped in a large cod net off the coast of Newfoundland.

many countries there are national parks and reserves set aside for the protection of wildlife. International efforts are now being made to reduce habitat destruction and prevent trade in endangered plants and animals and their products.

However, laws are not always obeyed and much work remains to be done. The future of the world is in our hands, as we exercise more control over what happens than any other species. If we fail, the world could become an uninteresting, barren and, perhaps, uninhabitable place. We owe it to ourselves and all the other species with which we share this planet to try and make sure that this is not allowed to happen.

Above: The best way to help a species or group of species to survive, is to preserve the habitat in which they live. Here, conservation workers are planting a small wood of hazel trees to maintain a habitat suitable for woodland butterflies.

Left: A land iguana on Isabela Island in the Galapagos Islands gets a cooling shower. It is being collected by conservationists attempting to save the species from being wiped out by feral dogs (domestic dogs allowed to go wild). Only nine of the iguanas were found.

INDEX

ACKNOWLEDGMENTS

PHOTOGRAPHS

B. & C. Alexander: pages 43, 74, 75 top
Bruce Coleman Ltd.: pages 12 Jeff Foote; 17 N. Schwirtz; 19 top right Kim Taylor; 33 Kim Taylor; 39 top Jane Burton, bottom Peter Davey; 44 Stephen J. Krasemann; 47 top Alan Root, bottom Kim Taylor; 52-3 Hans Reinhard; 54 Frans Lanting; 57 Rocco Longo; 61 top Frans Lanting, right middle Kim Taylor; 62 Leonard Lee Rue III; 71 Hans Reinhard; 72 L.C. Marigo; 75 bottom Udo Hirsch
Oxford Scientific Films Ltd.: pages 10 Michael Fogden; 15 Animals Animals Zig Leszczynski; 19 top left Peter Parks; 24 Robert Tyrrell; 26 Anthony Bannister; 30 Fredrik Ehrenstrom; 34 Peter Parks; 36 Michael Fogden; 40 Mike Brown; 42 Doug Allan; 48 J.K. Burras; 51 David Macdonald; 58 Mantis Wildlife Films; 61 left middle Rudie H. Kuiter, left bottom Scott Camazine, right bottom Michael Fogden; 65 Michael Fogden; 66 top, bottom Michael Fogden

ILLUSTRATIONS

Garden Studios: pages 18-19, 37, 49, 50, 55, 56-57, 60-61 Roger Gorringe
Ian Fleming: pages 20-21 Brian McIntyre
Linden Artists: pages 8-9 Mick Loates; 12-13 Jane Pickering; 14-15 Mick Loates; 22-23 Phil Weare; 24-25 Derick Bown; 27 David Webb; 29 Mick Loates; 32-33 Stephen Lings; 34-35 Alan Male; 38 Stephen Lings; 40-41 Phil Weare; 43 David Webb; 45 Clive Pritchard; 46-47 Derick Bown; 52-53 Alan Male; 58-59 David Webb; 62-63 Stephen Lings; 64-65 David Webb; 66-67 Alan Male; 68-69 Phil Weare; 70-71 Jane Pickering; 73 Stephen Lings
The Maltings Partnership: pages 11, 16, 17, 26 bottom, 28 bottom, 31